A Habit of Service:

Cyndy dear,
It's not our eyes.
The photos are all
blurry! LOL
Enjoy,
Gail
12/31/2020

A Habit of Service:

MY CONVENT STORY

Nancy J Davis

ISBN-13: **9781979760300**
ISBN-10**: 1979760306**

Contents

Introduction

Memories abound—
laughter, tears, joys, sorrows, all
captured in a trunk.

MY CONVENT TRUNK IS IN the basement; its tray is falling apart. Once long ago I covered the inside with contact paper, which is now crisp enough to chip off in bite-size nibbles and look like potato chips ready for dipping. Its outside has been beaten by multiple moves—seven convent missions, my single's flat, and three homes since my marriage.

It contains the treasures of my life. My convent years. My early-parenting years. Travel. My journals. My life in a rectangular box!

It's traveled with me for fifty-nine years. Nothing holds my memories more than my convent trunk. Opening it after multiple latent years exploded those memories. Those convent years. The years of growing up.

Just like my trunk that had pieces of my life, convent and all, intermixing with each other, I approach this memoir similarly. I tell my thirteen convent years somewhat chronologically and sometimes thematically. Each chapter captures memories of a specific time or event or a way of being or thinking, all memories that have influenced my life and thus yours, my readers. My mom saved my early letters, and I have inserted some in the story and others in the appendix. As I read those early letters, I feel an ache for my family I had left behind. I focused my letter writing so they knew I was thinking about them. I worked hard to describe my peace and contentment, part of which, I am sure, was nurtured by my superiors, who encouraged maintaining a positive front to family and friends.

When my grandson, Foster, was eight, he was told I was a nun. My son, Steve, asked him if he knew what a nun was. Playful or not, Foster didn't hesitate. "Someone who knows 'none-thing,'" he said. I knew then, for Foster's sake alone, I had to tell my story. My grandson hadn't met any religious women. I thought about my own children, now in their thirties and forties. They actually knew little about religious life. Any Sister they had in grammar school was of retirement age and coping with the new Gen X generation. My children didn't know the vibrancy of the Sisters and their lifestyle as I knew it. Unlike me, they probably did not experience the inspiration nor feel the compassion and love that I felt from the Sisters.

In turn, they haven't been curious about the convent or my years in it. I have offered stories now and then but haven't gotten the "tell me more" vibe. My hunch is that as they get older, they will wonder more what the convent was all about and why their mom acted and thought the way she did.

I was a young, pious, innocent seventeen-year-old when I entered, thus syncing comfortably with convent ways—for years. I left feeling enriched and self-assured.

Many of my thirteen years were met with simplicity, striving for perfection, and accepting a lifestyle full of rituals and traditions intended to shelter those who committed their lives to the service of God. This way of doing things had centuries of success. I thrived in that security.

Vatican II and the societal upheavals of the late 1960s threatened all that. I changed with the times. Like a Godiva chocolate bar removed from its golden paper, the value of being nun needed to be redefined. As every woman who had made vows had to do, I had to ask whether I wanted to be part of this redefinition.

I thought about naming this memoir *The Nun Thing*, in honor of my grandson. My brother Bill offered *Before I Kicked the Habit*. In final draft, I decided my story, this journey, was about *A Habit of Service*. And then I was ready to publish.

May those who know *nothing* about the religious life of the past enjoy reading its traditions and be inspired by the commitment it called forth and the opportunities it provided for growth and discovery. And for those who know *some* things, may this story generate fond memories and feel the inspiration over again.

The Beginnings

In a sense who you are has always been a story that you told to yourself.
Now yourself is a story that you tell to others.

—GEOFF RYMAN

Nurturing a Vocation

If you don't turn around now, we just may get to where we are going.

—Native American saying

Becoming a nun was an encouraged option in the Catholic pre–Vatican II Church, and most everyone knew someone who was a nun. A vocation to become a Sister was described as a "special calling from God" for a chosen few. Often the "calling" was triggered by someone in religious life who picked you out as a possible candidate. There were 185 girls in my high-school graduating class. Eleven of us entered the convent. How did it come about that I was one of those few?

In grammar school at St. John the Baptist, Mother Immaculate came to our classroom and asked us to pray that young women would become nuns and hinted that maybe one of us would consider being one. "Fifty in 1950," she would echo. I shyly looked down so she wouldn't pick me out, yet her sincerity and gentle style seeded an invitation that sprouted as I grew into my teenage years. In high school, my young and vibrant teachers not only talked vocation; they lived it. And they encouraged "good girls" to become religious women.

I was a lonely teenager. Mom was sick. Dad was working. I was insecure. Dad's rule was powerful. I saw my future blocked by what I knew: After high school, I probably would find a job, possibly keep the clerk job at the

Boston Store and just get more hours. I'd marry early, probably to a Croatian who Dad would pick for me. Several of my classmates already were engaged. I wouldn't go to college. Dad didn't believe girls should go to college. That future wasn't feeling right. I didn't belong in that vision. I didn't like how Alice and Martha, my coworkers at the Boston Store, turned out; they were cranky old ladies. Mom and Dad's marriage was tumultuous at best. Marriage seemed like a burden, not a joy. I had not been attracted to any boy I knew.

It was easy to be drawn to the Sisters' lifestyle, especially comparing them to what I experienced at home. My Mom had spent much of her time in bed or at the doctor's since I was ten. We no longer danced in the kitchen, and we hardly shopped together; her answer to "How are you?" tumbled into descriptions of how sick she was, unwelcomed messages to a teenager who was exploring what she wanted to be when she grew up.

Most of the Sisters who taught me were young and vibrant: Sisters Alette, Margaret, Siena, Miriam Rose, Alberta, Micheleen, Joseph Clare, Cabrini, and Noel. Even the older Sisters like Sisters Benetia, Anna Marie, Deborah, Jean Marie, Julian Marie, Anita Marie, and Clarette inspired me by their kindness and dedication. And then there was the really old Sister Clementia, who we thought was a bit odd but also brought enthusiasm into the classroom. What teacher besides her could get away with having high-school girls climb imaginary airplanes and cross the continents as she graphically described the world's geography?

They smiled, they told stories, they emitted a fun spirit of living, and most influentially, they always seemed to have time for me, lots of it—after school, helping with projects, listening to music, talking about important things. I found from them the attention, love, and concern I didn't know I was seeking.

I wanted to be like them. I wanted to live that spirit. They became my confidants, especially Sister Margaret, my Latin teacher, and Sister Siena, my freshman homeroom teacher. My parents *blamed* Sister Margaret when I chose to enter the convent.

The Sisters' vibrancy and free-spiritedness was teasingly friendly and joyous. They set focus to my life. I was attracted. And I was convinced that my reward would be great in heaven to live a gift-giving way of love and service to God.

My Roots

All things come to the soul from its roots, from where it is planted.

—Teresa of Avila

It's probable that my Austrian and Croatian genes had something to do with my decision: Mom's side for their devout dedication and gentle spirit and Dad's side for their free spirit and rebellious nature.

My grandparents were adventurous. All four as teenagers left Europe on a boat, joining relatives who already found roots in Joliet, Illinois. Little is known as to how they met, but given the immigrant nature of Joliet, Croatians found Croatians, and Austrians found Austrians, and thus, another generation began.

It is known, so the story goes, that Mirko Polyak was quite a bragger, a quality his son, Tom, my father, would inherit. While courting Vincenca, Mirko took her up a small hill. "Vinnie," he said, as he spread a handkerchief across the vast and open land below, "This is mine, all mine." Grandma Vincenca didn't know he meant only his handkerchief until well after they were married. Although they both came across the Atlantic from northern Croatian towns, Bregi Radoboj and Mrkopalj, just one hour apart, they did not meet until they came to Joliet.

Similarly, Joseph Kump and his bride, Sophie, met in Joliet, coming from two small Austrian towns, Plösch and Skrill, just two hours apart, towns that, after World War II, became part of southern Slovenia.

Both sets of grandparents had large families. The Polyaks had fifteen children, ten of whom survived into adulthood; Dad was the fifth child, second son and third child to live. The Kump family had eight children, six who survived; Mom was the oldest. Both Mom and Dad were forced to be the sibling lead in their families, struggling with alcoholic fathers and overburdened mothers. Neither family had much, the majority of the income they had going to the local saloons. Both my parents were survivalists and pledged never to drink—they didn't. Dad's addictive tendencies turned toward work. Mom's into shopping.

People who knew Dad—customers, neighbors, and acquaintances— loved him. He was a successful businessman, trustworthy and quick witted, always ready to tell the next joke and engage his listener in the latest story he heard. At home he was withdrawn, tired from the multiple hours he put "on the job," having little interest in family activities. He was restless—the first to leave a party. Even in his early years, before building homes, his work at the steel mill and hauling coal drained him. It was only in his later years that Dad turned to baseball as a source of relaxation; he'd slump into his La-Z-Boy, feet up, and soon the rhythm of the television would have him fast asleep.

He was determined to make a good living for our family, a way of separating himself from his father. Dad never forgave Grandpa Mirko for taking away the first house he built, the one Dad planned to give his new bride. Dad went on to build many homes, most in Crest Hill, Illinois; he even had a street named after Mom, Alma Drive. During my growing-up years, Dad would build or remodel a home, we'd move in, and then he'd sell our new home to the first person who showed interest. Mom was not consulted; we lived in nine homes before I turned seventeen, most bicycle distance from each other. They were, though, far enough that we were forced to make new friends, including going to different schools. I went to three grammar schools, Cunningham, Chaney, now Chaney-Monge, and Saint John the Baptist.

Dad was a protective father and husband and controlled our activities. Mom felt obliged to be home to serve him lunch and supper, thus she wouldn't say yes to a ladies' luncheon or any day-out excursion. It took her years to learn to drive, and then she'd only go to the store and back. Before Louis Joliet

Mall, Mom found haven and release from family responsibilities shopping at the Boston Store and Goldblatts. We'd beg to go with her, especially to Goldblatts, because they had open bins of cookies where we could choose our favorites. It didn't take much to find out what she shared with Dad and what she didn't. Cookies were shared, but the new purse or earrings she bought for herself were not part of her show-and-tell. The bags were either stuffed in a closet or emptied and merchandise put away, far before he arrived home, a practice she continued, even after Dad's passing.

As bold and loud as Dad could be, Mom was timid and retiring. My greatest joy with her was during my early years where she would take me in her arms and dance around the kitchen. Her kingdom—the kitchen—she loved it. I remember the smells as my brother Tom and I walked in from school: chili, spaghetti sauce, chocolate cake, and other welcome embraces. I'm home!

But by the time I was ten, and after the birth of my second brother, Billy, she favored her bed, where she escaped from migraine headaches—way too frequent and overpowering. Even the brown powdered medicine wrapped in wax paper that the doctor prescribed didn't seem to help. I became Billy's caregiver. Mom's headaches continued and were compounded by other unidentified illnesses, one of which I was to understand later was depression. The doctor prescribed Valium.

Mom gave up trying to be accepted by the Polyak family. She got clear signals from her in-laws that Dad could have done better had he married a Croatian. She eventually decided the last thing she ever wanted to be was Croatian. We didn't go to Polyak-cousin parties and grew up hardly knowing that side of the family. The last of my grandparents to die was Grandpa Mirko; I was sixteen. Any reason to gather with them became less and less frequent.

Mom stayed close to her own siblings, especially Aunt Betty Lousher. They would talk nearly every day, and we always knew mom had a conversation with her because Aunt Betty would have offered a healing remedy for herself or for one of us. We tagged her as Doctor Lousher. Once Uncle Al retired, he would visit Mom every day, and they'd chat for hours. He'd come for morning coffee and often be there until Dad came home for lunch. Then, while Mom fixed lunch, the two of them would argue the political wrongs of the world. I wondered how Dad knew so much since he didn't read or watch the news. Mom's closeness with her family seemed to give her a comfort she didn't always feel in her own home.

There were times Mom didn't want to remember, but it seems her stories screamed to be heard. She told us about Grandpa's heavy steps coming up the wooden stairs to their second-floor apartment, which sat above the little grocery store Grandma ran. He'd come late for dinner and a fury of activity was set in motion to manage his raging needs. Mom was assigned to his well-being, sometimes going into the saloon to nudge him to come home. She feared most that staircase since she never knew what demands he would make. No member of the family was safe from his poisonous tongue.

Grandpa Kump died before I was able to remember him, but his memory lived in the depths of Mom's unhealed soul as she sadly told stories until her death.

I do remember the stairs. Attached to the back of the house, narrow, creeping wood, seasoned by the weather, they went straight to a small wooden porch, additionally creepy, that housed a small icebox. I remember the ice man shouldering two blocks of ice at a time as I would count how many drops would fall on his heels before he unloaded his burden. In good weather, he would give me ice chunks to soothe the heat.

Despite the unresolved hurts of her youth and Dad's demanding ways, Mom worked hard to give us a happy childhood. I was the first grandchild in her family. Mom's sisters, all teenagers when I was born, had to come to my birthday party, even though it was the day after Christmas. Aunt Betty would bake the chiffon cake and Mom the angel food cake, neither from a cake mix. That tradition went on for years. None of her sisters had any money, and so my gifts were recycled, many of them records. As they favored different kinds of music, I was given the discards, record albums from the big bands of Jimmy Dorsey and Glen Miller. I loved them and as a little girl danced to them all the time. My aunts didn't give me their Bing Crosby and Frank Sinatra records since they turned into *bobby soxers* who idolized Bing and Frank for years.

Since there was a gap of several years before my second and third brothers, Bill and Larry, came along, Mom and Dad and Tom and I were a bonded family of four for several years, living the longest in one house together, five years, 2323 Clement. Tom and I were outside as often as possible and always surrounded by lots of neighborhood kids. We'd play baseball and cowboys and Indians; we even had cowboy outfits to make our play more authentic. We'd build tents; we'd create homemade circuses and shows, which I loved to orchestrate. One time one of my tent-building exercises turned into a disaster. Trying to anchor a blanket under a trailer hook sitting in the back of the yard, I felt it slip and fall on my foot. I spent the summer with a sprained foot, unable to walk. The doctor said that had I broken it, it I would have healed faster.

Our shows were made up of dancing and singing and held in our unfinished basement, becoming a nice respite during the summer months since air conditioning wasn't in any of our homes. I'd make and sell for a penny my homemade recipe for graham cracker cookies: graham crackers spread with butter and sprinkled with graham cracker crumbs.

I had two special girlfriends growing up, JoAnn Witczak and Bev Zbaznik. We went everywhere together in high school. JoAnn drove us in her 1954 Chevy back and forth to school. We'd stop at the Prince Castle, just a block away from school, whenever we could save up enough money. My order was always a grilled cheese sandwich with mustard and pickles and a square "scoop" of orange sherbet. Sometimes we ate in the school cafeteria. I remember the three of us able to pull together five cents so we could share a bag of potato chips. Most days we brought our lunch; mine was peanut butter and jelly. We loved going to Saint Joseph's Park on a Saturday night; most times we hung around and felt the music and the atmosphere. None of the three of us were good dancers and were shy around boys.

I insisted that JoAnn spell her name with a capital "A" in the middle because I thought it was special, just like she was. She spells it that way even today. Little by little JoAnn and I just hung around together and became friends with other girls who were interested in the convent, Eleanor Harmon and Carol Rushing among them. They eventually went to the Benedictine's in Lisle and JoAnn and I to the Joliet Franciscans. We joined with two other classmates, Judy Yonke and Juanita Ujcik, and several girls who, as freshmen, had entered what they called the Aspirancy and periodically had classes with us. Among them are women who have become lifelong friends, Nancy Rubadue, Roberta Reynolds, and Marilyn Fearday.

It was also probable that being perfect, which seeded our family life, also led me to the convent. Children of alcoholics, both my parents tended to be overshadowed by the world outside, watching and monitoring every action. My brothers and I would hear often, "What will others think? Don't do anything that will embarrass us!" Perfection, coated with shame, was a high expectation. It conditioned Dad so much that even a pimple on my teenage face would have to be removed immediately at his hand. That he followed the bus I was on and read my diary and then threw it away were means he used to ensure that I was staying on a right and proper track. The attraction to the convent to live "the perfect life" in God made all the sense I needed, to leave one controlling atmosphere for another, especially one that had such high goals—love of God and service to others—no longer just "What will the neighbors say?" I took literally and strived to "be perfect as your heavenly Father is perfect" (Matt. 5:48). The convent seemed to be the likely choice to grow in perfection and yet safe from my dad's definitions of perfection.

Larry, Tom and Bill with me: Summer 1958

The Motherhouse

~~⌒~~

It wasn't exactly love at first sight, but it was deeper than that.
A sense of belonging to a place I never knew I wanted but somehow
always needed. It was a home that carried a heartbeat.

—Nikki Rowe

Long before zip codes, a large white stone building sat at the diagonal corner of Plainfield and Taylor in Joliet, Illinois, a monument of strength and stability. Built in 1881, it cuts off the eastern end of a large piece of property that would have ended in a triangle had the building not rested there. Its address was 520 Plainfield Road, Joliet, Illinois, so it soon was known only as "520" or "the Motherhouse" and was the residence and business offices of the Sisters of Saint Francis of Mary Immaculate for over 120 years. It was to become my home and my anchor for 13 years.

In 2004, the University of Saint Francis, which sits on the western end of the same property, bought the Motherhouse and enhanced the building's history by naming the front offices the University's Welcome Center. They brought color and art into the hallways; they transformed room by room into a student-friendly environment, including the dormitories and dining rooms. A large Welcome sign graces the bottom of the wide stone staircase that leads to the entrance. Two hitching posts to drape the reins of horses still stand at the foot of the staircase, reminding all of the building's rich history.

On September 14, 1958, twenty-six spirited women, most right out of high school, walked up that grand staircase to begin the Franciscan way of life as *religious women, sisters,* or *nuns,* three words used by many interchangeably to describe those dedicating their lives to God. I was one of them. Over eight hundred other women had taken the same steps before us. The white stained-glass doors, framed by golden stone and elevated by fourteen concrete stairs sent excitement through my soul.

I climbed those stairs to enter into a life of love and service. Although over fifty years ago and after many life changes, that warm feeling fills my heart each time I ascend those stairs.

The feeling wasn't the same for my dad and mom as they trailed behind me that day and for many years thereafter. They were hoping at every moment that I would turn around and change my mind. I didn't.

We were guided into the front parlor, which I found out later also served as the receiving room to wake deceased Sisters. A slight smell of flowers lingered. The sun cast a shadow between the heavy drapes exaggerating the height of the windows. I was excited and yet concerned for my parents, who were extraordinarily quiet, so that whatever kind of welcome we received and who did it is far gone from memory. Quickly, I was separated from my parents and taken to a room to dress in my postulant clothes and to prepare for the entrance ceremony. Black serge dresses neatly hung in rows, well pressed and smelling of dry-cleaning, or was it moth balls? I wondered how many wore the dress I chose before me.

Tables held white-collared black capes and white-banded black veils—labeled with each person's name. I scanned quickly and there was *Miss Nancy Polyak,* my name, and what I would be called for the next year. "This is for real," I said to myself. "I'm actually here." Whew! I hadn't been the last to arrive; it looked like six more were still coming. It took a long time for my parents to get in the car and when my dad had just sat there, not starting the engine, I feared we'd never arrive.

Finally there, I had a slight fear that my parents, who were sent to put my trunk in the storage room, wouldn't come back. They were to go around the corner to drop off the large black trunk Mom and I had been filling for months. That trunk was to become the stable component of my life, containing everything I owned and cherished. Following the pre-convent checklist, I had put plain white cotton undergarments, which left no hint of shapeliness, two black slips, black stockings, old-lady-looking black shoes with laces and thick one-and-a-half-inch heels, a sewing kit, a manicure set, and basic toiletries. Although not on the list, I nestled a five-inch circular mirror between the clothes. I couldn't imagine being mirrorless. Mom and I had sewn assigned labels on everything that would be going through the laundry. All I was to own was in the trunk, and that trunk would travel from mission to mission with me.

I left everything from my first seventeen years behind, and much to my mom's distress, I had thrown away, given away, or burned everything that would not be going with me. I did this to follow literally the Gospel message, as centuries ago Saint Francis of Assisi did when he stripped himself naked in front of his father and walked away from all worldly things: "Sell what you have and give to the poor. You will then have treasure in heaven. Then, come and follow me" (Luke 18:22).

My sense of "letting go" had started in high school when I joined the Saint Francis Club. I took to action the messages of Saint Francis, giving away everything of value, even my collection of baseball cards, which had I saved would probably have paid for my firstborn's college education. I burned my high-school scrapbooks that so methodically captured my memories. I even wrote a "last will and testament," which created much sadness for my parents.

My reasons for entering the convent were many. I entered to save my dad's soul. He denounced God, faith, and any type of religion. I entered to serve God. I entered, not admitting at the time, to free myself of Dad's controlling style, which day by day and year by year in the convent lifted and freed me despite the convent's multiple rules.

On that crisp end-of-summer day, the sun was bright and the leaves were beginning to change colors. The echoes of autumn were creeping in—in ways that suggested to my family that a death of an era had come. I didn't realize that I broke my dad's heart and his dreams for his only daughter. I didn't know the tears of sadness that would fill the family household. My then seven-year-old brother Billy told me years later that he cried every day for a year. He told me that he and Dad would drive by the convent daily to see if they could get a glimpse of me on the campus, and once in a while, they did.

When my family left on that September day, I looked around my new surroundings and saw a few tearful classmates. My heart was leaping, but I contained my smiles inside. I was where I wanted to be. I knew little of what was to come. I just knew I was giving myself blindly and fully. Deep down I knew I would find the happiness and fulfillment I so much sought.

The Motherhouse
520 Plainfield Rd.
Joliet, Illinois

The First Year: The Postulancy

1958–1959

There is something charming and peculiar about a beginning.
You feel it, like the change of seasons, from winter
to spring, from spring to summer.
You feel it; the new blood pumping inside your veins.
You feel it: a thousand butterflies fluttering
around your fingers to help you fly.
You feel it: on your lips, when you smile at the absurdities
of life that suddenly make perfect sense.
You smile…Because in every beginning, there is a rebirth.
Because in every beginning, there is a layer
of you that you just discovered.
A layer you forgot was buried in you all this time.
You smile because you are reminded of the immensity of fate.
You smile because suddenly you feel so small and you like it…
This life is beautiful.

—MALAK EL HALABI

Redefining How to Live

The soul should always stand ajar.

—Emily Dickenson

In a large household of women who valued the sacredness of silence, discipline, and respect, rules were abundant. The morning after families left, Sister Zita, our postulant mistress, called us together for the first of weekly assemblies. We had met briefly the night before to get direction on how to get through the evening and early-morning prayer. As I remember, her first talk went pretty much like this:

> I see you made it through your first night of Grand Silence, [there were a couple of giggles] and almost all of you got through our morning ritual.

Silence grabbed the room as we awaited news about the word "almost." It never came. Her tone turned into a highly prepared talk, and it became apparent that a two-way conversation was not how these assemblies would run.

> Among all the girls in your high school class, you were called, and you responded. This year is a testing year to see how well you can live the disciplined life of a woman dedicated to God. [Oh boy.] If, at the end

of the year, you still feel the calling, you petition to become a novice; the congregation reviews your request. If, at any time, you don't believe you should be a Sister, or the congregation thinks it better that you live in the world, you are free to leave.

Do not talk about your feelings with each other since you don't want to burden others with doubts or bring about sadness. Any conversations around your vocation are to be had with me or your confessor.

Today I will give you some basic expectations. Some of our practices may feel awkward, but eventually you will get use to them. We have many Sisters at the Motherhouse, and living together under one roof demands certain respect and order from all of us.

This year you will be able to write to your family once a month. You receive mail every Saturday. I read both your incoming and outgoing mail. [Oh dear, hope my dad doesn't curse.] I encourage you to be pleasant and upbeat in your letters, even if you are homesick. And besides, by the time the letters reach your family, your feelings usually change and you have worried your family unnecessarily.

You already were introduced to Grand Silence, which you will learn to cherish. It begins at 9:00 p.m. as you prepare for bed [We go to bed at 9:00 p.m. every day?] and ends at breakfast. Most days we carry silence over until recreation at 6:00 p.m. Those days you may talk in class and at times when it is practical and prudent to speak. We do not engage in useless chatter. On holidays and holy days, we speak with respectful conversation all day.

As you experienced today, we rise at 5:00 a.m. with the sound of the chapel bell, are in Chapel by 5:30 a.m. for meditation following by the chanting of the Office at 6:00 a.m. [Gulp!] Rise quickly and silently and come directly to chapel.

Besides keeping silent, when you walk, teach your eyes to remain downward, so you stay open to the God within you. We call it *custody of the eyes*, and you will find it won't take long to adjust to quieting your eyes.

Swinging your arms is frivolous, and you should place your hands under your cape; it helps you remember to cast your eyes down.

We conserve energy. You bathe each night as you did last night [Not sure I will ever get used to a bowl and washcloth] and shower once a week. You will get your postulant outfit cleaned twice this year, so you are responsible to keep it neat and clean. [Did I bring spot remover?] You will, of course, change your white collar weekly. If you have an accident, come to me for permission for early cleaning.

Speaking of permission, you can go freely to class, chapel, and daily prayer walks outside, but you are to ask permission to go anywhere else.

Laundry is on Saturday morning, and you are responsible to drop your clothes off Friday night in the laundry bins. After Saturday dinner, you will find your clothes in a bin with your number on it. Someone of you asked why the numbers are so different. One may have a number in the eight hundreds, another in the forties. We recycle numbers, so if you have a low number it means one or more Sisters has had your number before you. Pray for her soul. Ask her for her blessings. Does everyone know your number? Is your number sewn onto your clothes?

I looked around, thinking of the number of hours it took Mom and me to finish that task. Miss Elaine timidly shook her head no. Sister Zita assured her we'd all pitch in and help. She continued her directives.

We show respect to our superiors, so when Mother Borromeo or a priest walks in the room, we stand to greet them. You do not have to stand for me.

Finally, for today, I want to discourage particular friendships. Some of you entered with classmates and friends you have known for a long time. [I took a quick peek at JoAnn, whom I had known since we were little. We had been so often together in high school that JoAnn was often called Nancy and I JoAnn. *This one is going to be tough*, I said to myself.] Your life now is one dedicated to God and, thus we discourage you from singling out one or two people with which you spend your time. In true charity, you are to be friendly to all.

I know there are other practices that I have not shared with you today, and I will review them at other weekly assemblies. If you have any questions, my door is always open.

Really odd, my brain said—all these rules—but this *is* the convent. And although I was escaping my dad's controls, I was putting new ones on me. The difference was big—I was *choosing* them, and I was doing them for a cause bigger than myself.

Sister concluded, and we were sent off in silence to unpack and prepare to have a Motherhouse tour in thirty minutes. *It's OK*, I said to myself. Dad ran a tight ship at home. The difference was that I didn't always know the Dad rules until I violated one; here they were spelled out in detail. I was used to being monitored and living in fear of punishment, and after all, they won't kick me out because I soil my dress, will they? I looked deeper inside. *I am here to serve God, and if keeping these somewhat awkward rules is the way to do it, I will do this. Many have done it before me. I can do this.*

The bonus was that there were other things I wouldn't have to deal with anymore. When I was sixteen and began working downtown at the Boston Store, I would take the bus and get off a block before, stop in for Mass at Saint Mary Magdalene, and walk to the store, arriving just in time to join Alice and Martha in the men's department.

One day, as I climbed the stairs to the church, I noticed a red truck turn the corner and pick up speed, almost as if it was trying to hide from my sight. I saw it again several times and finally had the courage to confront my dad. "Are you following me?" He gave me a spontaneous no, and that ended the conversation. After that I saw that red truck near and around at other times— when I went to Saturday night dances at Saint Joseph's Park with JoAnn and Bev; I even saw it one time when JoAnn and I stopped at Prince Castle for ice cream after school.

Another day I overheard my mom telling Aunt Betty that their younger sibling was having an affair. Mom confided that Dad found out because he was following her. Mom added that his own sister, Kathie, ran away from home in her teens and became a strip-club dancer in Chicago. I guess that made him unable to trust even his young daughter, who, good grief, was thinking only of running to God.

Despite the tight convent rules, including many quiet hours, combined with early waking and retiring, I was liking my days in community and not feeling as homesick as so many of my classmates were. By January three girls had left, and three new girls came in; those three were older and more mature than the rest of us. One had been engaged to be married, something that was hard for me and our less-experienced girls to grasp.

My mom and other family members were diligent writing to me, and I wish I would have kept their letters. Part of my spirituality was rooted in abandoning things, and I guess throwing away letters was part of letting things go. Mom didn't feel that way, and she kept many of my early convent letters, all handwritten and ink fading, which I discovered when putting her estate to rest. I include them in this memoir.

What follows is the earliest letter I wrote that Mom kept. Most of those early letters carried over the mantra I was taught to put on every piece of paper since grammar school—JMJF: Jesus, Mary, Joseph, and Francis. This practice was to keep them always present with us.

JMJF
Fall 1958
Dear Mom and Dad,

I feel right at home here. For one thing, most the building is being remodeled, so the smell of fresh paint and dust is perfect for a contractor's daughter.

Oh, Dad, I haven't had turnips or sauerkraut as of yet. The food has been delicious. I'm always full…and content.

Mom, prepare yourself, I had my first soft-boiled egg this week… and I'm still living. In fact, since I have them every day. I'm beginning to enjoy them. Was the shock too great for you???? Only kidding, but in the convent we learn to take the good with the bad and then the bad doesn't seem so bad after a while.

Tell Bev thanks for the letter. I enjoyed it—especially the different colors of ink.

Just this minute I was given a package—it was from Mrs. Witczak— candy. Wasn't that thoughtful of her?

Sister Zita was talking to your Sister the other day, Billy. She said you're doing very well. This is the first year she is teaching.

How is your hot rod, Billy? I bet it's the best in the neighborhood.

How do you like your new bedrooms, boys? Is mine changed into a boy's room yet, Tommy, or is it frilly?

Mom says you can't sleep on such a big bed, Larry. I hope you don't have too many bumps.

Has our house been sold yet Dad? Have you got a lot picked out?

Saturday, Mom, was my first time to skate with the nuns. All of the postulants went out to the Academy. It was our initiation ceremony, as they called it. Sister Margaret was Master of Ceremonies during the skating program. I had a few skates with her—in fact I skated with all of them. I only fell twice on the slippery floor. Sister Louis Paul met the floor four times. We had a riot.

Afterwards we said our afternoon prayers and then went outside by the wishing well for a wiener roast. It was all such fun…but we appreciated our beds that night.

On Saturday morning we worked in the laundry, folding clothes and mangling—our mangles are much different than the one we have at home, Mom—much bigger and hotter. Sunday is a day for leisure; we listen to records while we study, sometimes write letters and we enjoy ourselves.

You asked me what I do all day. Here is my weekday postulant schedule:

5:00   Time to rise
5:30   to chapel I go

6:15   *Mass*

7:00   *I do my "charge." Every day I clean our study room*

7:30   *Breakfast with spiritual reading*

8:00   *to Tower Hall and school I go*

11:30   *dinner once again*

12:30   *we talk with our mistress*

1:00   *back to school or study*

3:30   *coffee break—more food*

3:30   *free to do what we wish, usually we're outside*

4:30   *prayer in chapel*

5:30   *supper time*

6:15   *recreation; we play games, sew and have a laughing good time*

6:40   *we say our special prayer of the church: the Office*

7:30   *study time*

9:00   *to bed we go*

9:45   *lights out*

It's a great life! Well, my paper is running out, I'll have to sign off. Write soon.

With all my love,

Nancy

Our Postulant Class of 1958
I am in the upper row, third from the left

The Hallways and Stairs

$\sim\!\!6$

It's not a question of conquering a summit previously unknown,
but of tracing step by step a new pathway to it.

—GUSTAV MAHLER

LONG HALLWAYS, LINOLEUM-COVERED STRETCHES OF quiet, whispered hardly
a sound even though hundreds of feet walked them every day. We wore soft
rubber heels. Our pre-convent checklist had directed that any hard heels were
to be replaced with soft ones. One classmate forgot, and her heels changed
in a day—a highly valued living requirement. A major pathway had swinging doors, which we learned quickly had to be approached from the right,
slowly and cautiously so our seventeen-year-old stampeding gait would not
knock over the ninety-year Sister coming from the other direction. One day, I
walked right into the swinging door, forgetting to gently open it. No one was
on the other side. Whew! Loose tooth? Fortunately that tooth, already a false
one replaced in a similar accident when I was ten, was quite sturdy. No damage. I learned that custody of the eyes could be a safety hazard and needed to
keep eyes down while keeping senses alert to space and distance.

Beige colored—most hallways fairly empty of inspiration—one hallway
displayed the former Mother Superiors, also called Superior Generals, appro-
priately, where serious, smileless faces, fully clothed in nineteenth-century
garb, reminded us of the serious nature of our lives as women of God.

There was no need for planned exercise since navigating the stairs and hallways called for its own level of stamina. Of course, not yet twenty, I didn't think twice about all the walking and climbing.

All pathways led to the chapel, which was in the center of the building. Mother Superior's office was steps away from the chapel, and I was grateful when her door was shut. At other times I was pleased to practice custody of the eyes because I had no desire to catch her attention. She was a foreboding presence, Mother Borromeo was, at least in the eyes of a young girl eager to fulfill her dream and who had had her as her principal at Saint Francis Academy.

At the end of the chapel corridor was the entrance to the Postulancy. There were two large rooms, one a study room and the other a recreation room, more beige in color. Between them was a washroom, the postulant mistress's office, and an emergency exit.

It was easy to know which room the mistress favored—the study room. We never talked in there. Most of the time, in the recreation room, red-flushed, Sister Zita would hold her hands to her ears, removing one of them periodically to rest a finger on her lips. "Shh," she'd say, "too loud," as our voices met the open chambers of a room that had no soundproofing. Of course, what could she expect, unleashing twenty-plus teenagers for open conversation one hour a day?

Family Visits

~~&~~

Smile at each other. Make time for each other in your family.

—MOTHER TERESA

ANTICIPATING FAMILY, VISITING FAMILY, AND saying good-bye are almost a numb blur. Our postulant mistress encouraged us to give a cheerful front. "Your family didn't travel to hear sad stories or see an unhappy daughter. Let the joy of Jesus shine through."

Everyone dressed in his or her finest clothes, setting up an uncomfortable engagement, especially for my little brothers. The visits were awkward since we sat around in a circle, something we never did at home. "How are you?" only takes a short time. "What have you been doing?" I answered that question a lot in my letters, so I tried to get my guests to talk. Dad would say he is building a house, end of description. Mom described her latest ailment, and my two school-bound brothers thought school was "OK." My sweet little baby brother wasn't sure about me. After all the hugs and love I gave him his first year, I left him.

When Aunt Betty and Cousin Mary Ellen joined them, I could always count on them bringing enough cheerfulness for all of us. Aunt Betty had a knack for asking questions that opened up conversation, and time went by much faster. "Is it what you expected?" she would ask. "Oh yes, and more," I would answer.

I liked when we could be outside on the convent grounds so that at least the boys could run around. The atmosphere felt freer and seemed to encourage a more relaxed interaction. At home, especially on Sundays, I remember hanging out in the living room. Dad in his La-Z Boy would be reading the paper and snoozing; he'd put on a new pair of jeans to get the week started right, and they would not see the laundry until Saturday. Brother Tom usually was in his room reading or out with friends. Billy would be running in and out of the kitchen to grab a bite to eat, and baby Larry was asleep. There would be a rump roast in the oven surrounded by potatoes and carrots. This lazy, comfortable family gathering only began after Mom took the two older boys and myself to church. Dad stayed home with the baby; before Larry, Dad stayed home too. Sunday was the one day of the week where Mom tried to stay out of bed and be more present with the family.

Aunts Betty (with Larry) and Edie and Cousin Linda

Ten minute visit with cousin Mary Ellen and
brother Bill on their Communion Day.

The Campus

The happiest is one who learns from nature the lesson of worship.

—RALPH WALDO EMERSON

WALKING AROUND CAMPUS, I HAD mastered the art of custody of the eyes so well that I didn't notice if Dad's truck went by, and only in letters did I hear they spotted JoAnn or me. The only peek my family could get was on the south end where concrete driveways ran around the building. Dad did find another way, the one he took to drop off my trunk, a private and more intimate entrance where spottings were more promising.

The acreage surrounding the convent was vast, serene, and inviting. I loved my late-afternoon walks, and no matter the weather, I found myself outside. Our winter wear was a long black wool mantle that draped over our clothes like a large blanket. A black wool scarf and gloves complemented its coziness. Usually the mantle kept me warm unless there was a strong wind. No matter how much I wrapped and rewrapped myself, the spinning wind would find its way through the eight-inch arm slits set on each side of the mantle. On those days my walks were shorter.

On the far west side of the campus stood the all-girls' College of Saint Francis, now coed and called the University of Saint Francis. Between the college and the convent lay well-manicured, tree-lined grounds, guarded at the north by a tall fence.

The campus was deliciously green most seasons, inviting a fresh and wholesome breeze, especially welcomed in the summer when the weight of woolen clothes sought relief.

One of the oldest tree species in the world, the Ginkgo tree, stood with elegance and grace in the middle of the campus, shared only by the Blessed Virgin grotto, which it shadowed and protected. I loved the Ginkgo's fan-shaped leaves, richly green in the spring and radiantly yellow in autumn. Visiting the center of campus became a landmark stop. I could honor the Blessed Virgin by saying a decade or two of the Franciscan Crown and then talk to the tree. I found both inviting companions in my otherwise solitary walks. In the summer when I returned back to the Motherhouse, one of my first stops would be the Ginkgo tree.

Watching Ginkgo's buds burst in spring must have inspired this article that was printed in the college newspaper, the *Interlude.*

Spendthrift in spring

King Midas, your days are over—no more miserly hibernating days, hiding the earth under vaults of snow.

God, the Almighty Spendthrift, has swept you off your throne. He has opened nature's pocketbook for lavish spending.

A heaven-rocking thunder saw your end. And the world felt the treasure tinkle on lakes and cracked soil.

There was a sudden azure splendor in the sky. Bleak and dreary clouds scudded away, leaving a chuckle in fluffy pillows.

And everywhere He wills, nature is spilling richest green. Rusty trees and sagging ivy gain youthful beauty from this ageless Spender. Blades of grass struggle but little to don an armor of lovely green. And to set it off in royal color, the Extravagant One tosses thousands of golden dandelion coins throughout the land.

New life is sown everywhere. Millions and millions of seeds, winnowing through the air, scatter hope to barren lands. Newly running brooks make fresh abodes for wayward fish.

Wherever He goes, He gives a golden smile to a weary land. The land in turn sings along with the bird: It's Spring!

–Sister Victor Marie, O.S.F.

The Interlude, April 21, 1961. Image courtesy of the Laverne and Dorothy Brown Library Archives, University of St. Francis, Joliet, IL

College

The more that you read, the more things you will know.
The more that you learn, the more places you go.

—Dr. Seuss

CLASSES IN COLLEGE WEREN'T EASY for me. Being twelfth in my high-school class, I had earned an academic scholarship to college, but my academic prowess of high school didn't seem to translate into college. I believe I did as well as I did because of the disciplined study time in our convent routine. Yet I found myself conditioned by my upbringing.

Critical thinking hadn't been encouraged in our household. Obedience was. We lived in fear with, "Wait until your dad comes home." When I was sixteen, I disagreed with him, probably in typical teenage style, and was met with a slapped face. I wasn't asked my opinion on family matters.

Reading wasn't allowed. Dad bragged that he never read a book in his life. I still hear him saying, "Get up off your lazy ass, and do something worthwhile." I felt sneaky and self-serving if I was reading and cherished the time when I could say, "It's homework." Despite Dad's attitude and maybe because of it, Mom became an avid reader, grabbing liberating opportunities whenever she could.

These underdeveloped skills didn't function well when Sister Beatrice, my English professor, would ask, "What did Edgar Allen Poe mean when he said,

'All that we see or seem is but a dream within a dream!'?" or "What might Robert Frost mean by 'Freedom lies in being bold'?"

The earliest version of published cheat sheets, *Cliff Notes*, were just coming out, and I'd see a classmate or two sneaking a look in the yellow and black booklets. I yearned to get my hands on them, especially for Shakespeare. I had to rely on my own thinking skills or lack thereof.

When I'd catch Sister Beatrice scanning in my direction, my eyes slipped to the text, and I'd feel a stammering of words even before I was asked to speak. Her response to me often was, "Think harder," or "Can anyone give a more relevant theory?" Her comments on my papers were as harsh: "I am determined to get you to think…and write."

Sister Beatrice was chair of the English department and seemed to favor assigning herself to all British-based literature classes and especially those with young Sisters in attendance. I took several classes from her. I earned only C's in her classes. It must have been my stubbornness that stopped me from changing my major, along with a sampling of other teachers who only gave me A's. Eventually my years in college balanced out.

I had Sister Seraphim for journalism and, maybe because of rather than despite, her astute ability to red mark my work, I learned to write. She was encouraging. I became a member of the journalism staff and published articles in the college newspaper. See Appendix B.

As you might guess, I didn't find metaphysics and logic classes easy either. Sister Helen Marie entertained while encouraging us to identify a fallacy and offer other ones, similar to this one: "Penguins are black and white. Some old TV shows are black and white; therefore some penguins are old TV shows." Within that playful environment, I enjoyed offering my thoughts. Although I was stymied many a time, my answers were considered part of the discussion rather than right or wrong.

All my preparatory classes for teaching with Sisters Charles Marie and Ambrose geared me up; they were practical and useful, and I flourished. The instructors brought so much enthusiasm to the profession that I could hardly wait until I was in the classroom myself.

When it came to taking finals in my major, I was teaching at Saint Pascal and spent weeks into months studying for the exam that would come when back on campus that summer. I built large charts identifying key themes, authors, and works and hung them on the back of my bedroom door. For the first time in my convent years, I had my own bedroom, and it helped a lot since I learned while talking to myself as I tried to memorize relevant information.

I was over-prepared, yet barely passed. I didn't schedule my time so that I'd have enough time for each question and over-answered the first few questions, leaving little time left for the later questions. It was hardy "lesson learned," and later when I prepared graduate students for comps, I drilled the need for time management.

The Second And Third Years: The Novitiate

1959–1961

The call to stillness is an invitation to draw close to God.

—Anonymous

Veni Spousa Christi

꧁

Come, bride of Christ, receive the crown
which the Lord has prepared for you for all eternity;
for whose love you have shed your blood.
And you will enter into the Paradise among the angels.
Come, O you my chosen one, and I will set my throne within you:
so shall the King have pleasure in your beauty.

WITH EYES CAST DOWN, DRESSED in identical simple veils and white organdy wedding gowns, I, with my classmates, processed the three blocks from the Motherhouse to the cathedral on a sunny, warm August 13, 1959, on way toward our next level of commitment—to become a novice. Each of us carried a small bouquet of flowers and were told to keep our eyes cast down as we walked.

I no longer would be postulant, Miss Nancy, dressed in a mid-calf serge black dress with a Peter Pan white collar cape, topped with a white band and sheer black veil that draped over my dark-blond hair. I would never have to curl my hair again. I would be getting a new name. I was becoming a bride of Christ. I *was* a bride of Christ. As the procession entered the cathedral, the choir began "Veni Spousa Christi," Come Bride of Christ.

This long dream of mine was real now. I wasn't a Sister as a postulant; I was a candidate. Now I would be one step closer to becoming a real Sister. I was at peace and yet fully excited. I would be donning the brown habit of the Sisters of Saint Francis of Mary Immaculate.

I was wondering what effort Mom had expended to get Dad to come. I warned her that the ceremony would be long. Dad had to know what he was getting into. I looked up to scan the church. Were they even there? It was quite full since not only were postulants becoming novices, but novices were making their first profession, called simple vows, which lasted three years, and finally those completing their simple vows were making their perpetual vows—about seventy-five of us total, each of us to receive one-on-one attention at the altar.

I expected that Mom would be wearing pink, her favorite color. Her hat would have pink flowers and veiling. Dad would be in a tan sport coat and brown pants and, if fully persuaded, wearing his tan-and-brown-striped tie. Next to them would be three wiggling boys, ages fourteen, eight, and two, who would be ready to go home before the ceremony actually started. Would Mom make them wear sport coats and ties? Maybe Mom would leave Larry, my littlest brother, with a babysitter. Yet her babysitter, me, was in the convent, and I hadn't heard if I had been replaced.

The click of our white pumps walking down the cathedral aisle stepped in rhythm with the music; it was odd to hear the sound of our walking since the rubber heels of our convent shoes silenced that sound. We kept a two-person distance between each other. Never very rhythmic, I feared I wouldn't stay in step and possibly tumble.

I was excited to be so close to Bishop McNamara when my name was called. His face was so rosy red, I wondered if he had just been out on the golf course. "Nancy Polyak, from this day forward you will be called (I sucked air in) Sister Victor Marie." I wanted to spin, jump, and shout yahoo, but instead I bowed to the bishop, and a Sister gave me a bundle of clothes.

For months before the ceremony, I practiced writing my Sister name, similar to other young girls fantasizing their future. I only wanted *Sister Victor Marie*—my dad and mom's middle names. It was common to choose a family name, so given my dad's hesitancy about my vocation, I hoped Reverend Mother would take that under consideration. I knew both Mom and Dad would be pleased if I got it.

Although my folks never said anything about my name, I felt exceptionally proud to carry their names. Only after Mom died did I find we didn't know Mom's official name. On her birth certificate, it was not Alma Marie, but Alma Mary.

Years later when opportunity presented itself, I again went back to Nancy Polyak, *Sister* Nancy Polyak, and I figured my dad would be even more pleased. Being a Polyak was important to Dad, and he instilled in us a deep pride: "You are a Polyak! Always remember that, and keep me proud." Again, Mom and Dad never said anything.

My living in the convent just did not make Dad proud. Marrying a Croatian and having loads of kids would have. In fact one of the first actions Dad took when I did leave the convent was to take me to a Croatian community center to "meet some nice Croatian men."

Postulant after postulant stepped forth and accepted the bundle. We were ushered to a back room, where we quickly stepped out of our bridal gowns and into our brown habits. Our hair was coarsely cut so that it fit into the head gear, and we donned the veil. As true of many rituals in the convent, this was done in silence and reverence.

The ceremony was indeed long, and I could hardly wait to see if my family was actually there and had sat through the entire ceremony. Did they hear the bishop announce my name, Sister Victor Marie? Were they excited to just plain get out of church? I headed toward our assigned section of the campus grounds, and since we were out of church before our family members, I had a chance to find JoAnn and give her a hug. We both got the names we wanted; she was now Sister Maria Goretti.

They came. I saw Bill and Larry racing ahead, and this tall young man edging up behind them. My brother Tom had grown at least a foot since I saw him last, and when he said hello, his voice cracked. I gasped and couldn't help wondering what else I was missing by being away. Aunt Betty was there with my cousin, Mary Ellen, supportive as ever. I hugged and kissed all; we found our station for food and visited until time ended. My new clothes were uncomfortable, and I was concerned whether the coif covered all my hair, that the head band was on straight, and that I'd lift my back scapular when I sat so it wouldn't get wrinkled. If Mom and Dad said anything about how

I looked, I can't recall. I suppose I should have felt holy, but I didn't; I was so self-conscious that not much sank in that day.

"Brides of Christ" I am first on the right, upper row.

Procession to the Cathedral
In background, dad taking my picture; mom and Larry to his right

My grown-up brother Tom and me

The Habit

In my sweet little habit of brown
I walk through the halls up 'n' down
I am both happy and glad
To be thus gaily clad
In my sweet little habit of brown.

A PARODY TO "ALICE BLUE GOWN" was a favorite song I'd silently sing as I walked through our convent halls. Sister Anthony Marie, a community poet, paraphrased the words.

I was proud to wear the habit—a T-shaped woolen robe that was tightened at the waist with a white cord. The cord dangled down the side, displaying three knots that represented the three vows I would be taking: poverty, chastity, and obedience. Over the habit I donned a piece of brown fabric about two feet wide, touching the hem of the robe on both front and back. This was called a scapular and was mainly used, as I could figure, to hide our hands so that now we would not only practice custody of the eyes, but we would silence our hands under the scapular when we walked. Finishing the body part of the habit was a large circular brown fabric collar, anchored at the neck with a white celluloid band. Recently the fabric collar had replaced a hard, white celluloid collar that matched the neckband. My hair would be cut short with no sensitivity toward styling, and I would put on a coif, a starched white head and neck covering that resembled a Star Trek headdress; it would be pulled tight by strings and tied in the back. My forehead would be covered with a celluloid shield that would be kept in place by elastic around the back of my head. So from the back I would have looked like a bound mummy. From the front, only my face was without cover. Completing the habit was a veil, white while I was a novice and later black when I became professed. The veil was modified from earlier years when the wing span, supported by cardboard and inserted in a veil, could be thirty-six inches wide and block any view of the Sister from the side. In 1959, it had been reduced to about eighteen inches wide and fell to the back, so a Sister's face could be seen from the side, and she was able to drive.

We had no full-length mirrors, but the Three Oaks convent, named for the grand three oak trees that shaded the west entrance, glass doors served as one. Coming back from classes, I had ample opportunity to enter through those doors and would pause just to take in my image. I'd check for a stray hair that may have popped out and push it back under my coif (the head piece).

Keeping my hair covered and the coif neatly in place was a constant vanity. A properly dressed Sister wore a clean, starched coif, tightly pulled over her ears, with attached strings tied in the back. Sloppy was a loose and baggy coif, sometimes with ties showing. I didn't do sloppy and found there were consequences.

My ears stood out boldly and resisted the forced enclosed environment in which they were forced. I soon developed a sore on my right ear that turned into a blister that turned into an infection. This condition forced me to wear a loose coif while the sore healed. As soon as it healed, I was back wearing a tight one, only to deal with the same medical condition again. I don't remember how often I had a sore ear, but the repetition led me to have a permanent scar, a wound of honor as I see it today.

I enjoyed the rhythm of the rosary that hung from my waist, and I peacefully walked through the halls with my hands silently under my scapular. The rosary was not the usual five-decade rosary. It was called the Franciscan Crown and had seven decades that celebrated the major events Franciscans honored in the Blessed Virgin's life: the Annunciation, the Visitation, the Nativity, the

Visit of the Magi, the Finding of Jesus in the Temple, the Resurrection, and the Assumption and Coronation.

We were encouraged to say the Crown daily "for an increase of vocations." And to gain "plenary indulgence" by the recitation of the Crown "at any time and in any place." I loved saying the Crown during my outside daily walk. I'd find myself moving to the center of the grounds to pray in front of the Blessed Virgin's Grotto. I mark the seasons according to the Ginkgo tree that beautifully shadowed the Grotto.

Going up and down stairs took practice. Lift the front hem of the habit up to go up the stairs so as not to fumble; lift the back hem of the habit up to go down the stairs so as not to get it dirty. Besides the habit, one had to capture the scapular in the lift, lest that become the cause of dismay. In those early weeks, it was not uncommon to forget which way to lift the habit, and novices were seen fussing and fumbling trying to manage the extra cloth.

We learned too that housekeeping and laundry work demanded another level of habit care. We would take the side ends of the habit, make sure the scapular was tucked in, and lift the front of the habit hem to our waist and wrap around to the back, anchoring the two sides with a large pin. This habit lift made mobility easier and kept the habit cleaner. Keeping the habit clean was important since, like our postulant clothes, we could get it cleaned just twice a year. Wearing the habit pinned up helped abundantly in the summer when the heat raced through the laundry room and hallways at a hefty speed.

I loved my years in the habit—five of them were in what we called "the full habit" as I received it on Reception Day, albeit I donned a black veil and a large crucifix after the two years of the Novitiate.

Then Vatican II happened, and with it many attitudes about religious women changed. I will describe these changes later as they impacted my life on mission and eventually my vocation.

But for me on that August day in 1959 when I donned the habit for the first time, I was thriving and enjoying each day's simple routine, habit and all.

At the grotto; Gingko tree to the right.
Picture taken not on Reception Day, but later--on Profession Day

Canonical Year

 ⌒

For the wedding of the Lamb has come and
his bride has made herself ready.

—Revelation 19:7

Following our reception, we white-veil novices thrust ourselves into prayer and service. We were not allowed to study secular subjects nor visit with family and friends during this year. The rules of the church, canon law, strongly directed the responsibility of the novice:

> Novices are to be led to cultivate human and Christian virtues; through prayer and self-denial they are to be introduced to a fuller way of perfection; they are to be taught to contemplate the mystery of salvation and to read and meditate on the sacred scriptures; they are to be prepared to cultivate the worship of God in the sacred liturgy; they are to learn a manner of leading a life consecrated to God and humanity in Christ through the evangelical counsels; they are to be instructed regarding the character and spirit, the purpose and discipline, the history and life of the institute; and they are to be imbued with love for the Church and its sacred pastors. (Canon 652, 2)

As canon law directed, being a novice meant we were challenged to perfect the ways of religious life. "I will do this," I proclaimed to myself—I can give myself completely and, since I was far from perfect—yet—I would strive for perfection as the convent defined it. At eighteen and full of energy, I hadn't the humility of wisdom to understand anything more.

We said good-bye to our postulant mistress, Sister Zita, as she prepared for another loud group of postulants coming in less than a month. My excitement of becoming a habit-wearing woman who was now called a Sister far exceeded any regrets of losing Sister Zita. I was ready to move forward, although I feared the well-seasoned, serious-faced novice mistress, Sister Anacleta; she was far older than Sister Zita and definitely more threatening. And I had learned that the overseeing mistress was like a sergeant in the army—follow directions or suffer the consequences, but all for the sake of becoming a *good* Sister, worthy of being a bride of Christ.

We moved to the Novitiate, one floor up from the Postulancy, a repeat design—a silent study room and a recreation room.

Sister Anacleta emphasized that this year, as canon law stated, was to be a major testing year. We were to settle in and needed to take our commitment seriously. It might have been the one year of convent living that seasoned us, or Sister Anacleta herself, but we were no longer accused of being loud.

To help us be more cloistered from the world, our classes were taken right in the Novitiate study room. They consisted of Gregorian chant, Christian life and worship, Christian moral ideal, liturgical music, and the religious element in English poetry.

I grasped eagerly this canonical, contemplative lifestyle, selecting to say daily two prayer cards given me on Reception Day, one by a high-school history teacher, Sister Anna Marie, and the second by my freshman homeroom teacher, Sister Siena. Both were very special prayers in this year and took on even more meaning and challenge once I faced some difficult mission assignments, specifically Saint Boniface and Our Lady of Guadalupe.

Forever Thine

Vowed to Thy love, Thy livery I wear;
Into Thy Hands my future I resign:
Grant, then, I beg this earnest whispered prayer,

Lord, keep my loving heart forever Thine.
Paths may be steep; life's skies may not be fair:
Whether the sun be darkened or it shine—
Calvary or Thabor's heights, make this my prayer;
Lord, keep my loving heart forever Thine.
All through life's journey, Master, let me share
Thy hardships let Thy ways, Thy works be mine.
But in exchange, Lord, grant me this one prayer:
Lord, keep my heart forever Thine.

Learning Christ

Teach me, my Lord, to be sweet and gentle in all the events of life—
In disappointments,
In the thoughtlessness of others,
In the insincerity of those I trusted,
In the unfaithfulness of those on whom I relied.
Let me put myself aside,
To think of the happiness of others,
To hide my little pains and heartaches, so that I may be the only one to suffer from them.
Teach me to profit by the suffering that comes across my path.
Let me so use it that it may mellow me, not harden nor embitter me,
That it may make me patient, not irritable,
That it may make me broad in my forgiveness, not narrow, haughty, and overbearing
May no one be less good for having come within my influence. No one less pure, less true, less kind, less noble for having been a fellow-traveler in our journey toward Eternal Life.
As I go my rounds from one distraction to another, let me whisper from time to time, a word of love to Thee. May my life be lived in the supernatural, full of power for good and strong in its purpose of sanctity.

Grand Silence

Somewhere we know that without silence, words lose their meaning.

—Henri Nouwen

After a year of early to bed, early to rise, and not adding any noise during those sacred hours except the shuffle of soft slippers, our Novitiate was well practiced.

More privacy was introduced when we novices were to wear nightcaps so our heads would remain covered at all times. I have a hunch one of the reasons was so we wouldn't giggle at each other's harshly cut hair-dos.

Preparing for bed was a simple routine. We shared a dormitory with about fifteen others. A single bed and a small waist-height dresser with one drawer and two doors identified our space. A washing bowl sat atop the linoleum-covered dresser, and a towel rack hung to its side. Our bedroom space was called a cell, where a curtain was pulled tightly to the right side and could be pulled around the bed and cubicle entrance whenever we were there. At other times, the curtain remained open, and nothing was left on top the dresser except the washing bowl.

Showers were once a week, and daily bathing was relegated to the washing bowl. The first exercise of the evening was to fill my washing bowl with warm water. It didn't take long for us to pace ourselves so that we didn't have fifteen night-capped women standing in line to get water. We got our water from a regular-size sink and had to learn to hold the washing bowl at a certain angle so the water would come in and not pour out.

The last exercise of the evening was to empty the used water and fill it up with water for the morning. Many a winter morning, I'd wake to a bowl of water coated with ice. That bathing didn't take very long.

Night routine could be finished in twenty minutes, and lights were expected to be out in forty-five. Surprisingly it didn't take much to fall asleep, even in the summer when the sun was far from setting. Five o'clock came mighty early, and I took all the sleep I could get.

We were taught that wearing the habit was a graced gift, and thus when we put each piece of clothing on, we said a special prayer. Our prayer book gave us the following prayers, which I soon knew by heart:

At the signal of the bell for rising, after blessing myself:

> *Sweet Jesus, I salute Thy most loving Heart, and I offer Thee my own; enkindle it with the fire of Thy divine love. Amen.*

When putting on my shoes:

> *Grant, O my God, every step I take this day may be directed by Thy holy will, and bring me nearer to Thee. Amen.*

When putting on the religious habit:

> *I am unworthy, O my Jesus, to be clothed in the livery of Thy spouses; yet grant me the grace to wear it faithfully in a spirit of penance until death.*

When putting on the cord:

> *May this girdle remind me of Thy passion, O Lord, and urge me to do works of mortification and charity.*

When putting on the silver crucifix:

God forbid that I should glory, save in the cross of our Lord Jesus Christ, by whom the world is crucified to me, and I to the world.

When putting on the religious veil:

May this veil, my dearest Jesus, hide me from the world, and ever remind me of my consecration to Thy love and service.

I was grateful that there was no special prayer for putting on my coif since many a day the quiet response was "Ow" as I pulled the starched fabric over my blistering ear.

Grand silence didn't officially end until after the breakfast reading. After the meal blessing, a short biography of the saint of the day was read aloud as we passed the dishes served family style. Many days general silence was kept even after the readings, and official permission to talk wasn't given until recreation time at 6:00 p.m. It probably is fairest to describe our talking on silent days as transactional talking, talking needed so that tasks could be done effectively and efficiently. That level of talk included permission to ask and answer questions in college classes.

Chapter of Faults

You're in pretty good shape for the shape you are in.

—Dr. Seuss

BEFORE THE CATHOLIC CHURCH OFFERED general confession for the laity, religious communities had their own group confessions, called the Chapter of Faults. Monthly we assembled with our novice mistress for a Day of Reflection, which ended with Chapter. At the Chapter of Faults, we took our turns to accuse ourselves of a fault. I had two faults that I would rotate sharing—failure to use custody of the eyes (it was hard to curb my curiosity as to what was happening around me) and falling asleep during 5:30 a.m. meditation.

Rolling vibration of silent laughter made itself across the room when Sister Allison confessed she got angry with the sewing machine. Even our stoic novice mistress, Sister Anacleta, struggled to control herself. Laughter was not part of our solemn Chapter ritual.

During the month, if we committed some fault that couldn't or shouldn't wait to confess, we were expected to visit the novice mistress's office, kneel down in front of her, and admit our fault. The day I broke the living-room vase was during my second-year Novitiate right after Sister Cyrinus took Sister Anacleta's place. I nervously paced the office until I could go in. It turns out she seemed to be more nervous than I was and was just concerned that I'd clean it up completely. Sometimes, if serious enough, we'd kneel down in front of the novice mistress anywhere we could find her in the confines of the Motherhouse.

Punishments for such offenses ranged from "Don't do it again" to kneeling at the silent breakfast table to silently saying six Our Fathers with arms outstretched in chapel. My breakfast kneeling usually was assigned because I was too social—talking to someone during silent hours, and especially to college classmates, which was forbidden. I just couldn't not talk to former high-school friends, especially when they initiated the conversation. The kneeling was worth it, and I considered it a badge of friendship.

Chapter of Faults did not take the place of private confession. We were encouraged to go every other week. As a child I brought routine sins to the confessional: disobeyed my parents, was mean to my brothers, and told a lie or two. In the convent I didn't have those "sins" and don't remember what I had to confess, but I bet they were big, and I was humbled for committing them over and over again. White-haired, gentle Father Angelo was always waiting in the confessional. He was also our college professor during our first-year Novitiate, so I'm glad I didn't scandalize myself because maybe it could have affected my grade.

Convent Chores

Cleanliness is next to godliness.

—Ancient proverb

Part of being a canonical novice, the year we were sheltered from family and friends and took only religious-based college subjects, was being fully indoctrinated into serving the Motherhouse community as housekeepers, kitchen crew, and laundry maids.

Our novice mistress must have looked over the bunch of us and chosen Sister Lora and me for all the strong-armed jobs. I guess because we were the tallest and thus looked the strongest. Other jobs like dusting, ironing, and serving the Sisters in the refectory, the convent name for dining room, were left to the others.

Using the buffer to polish the halls was challenging. The janitor would wash and wax the linoleum, and Lora and I would take turns managing the buffer. It took the motion of both arms and hands to keep the vibrating going back and forth across the wide terrain, creating moon circles, moving to the walls, but not bumping into them. We buffed the halls every two weeks whether they needed it or not. They never seemed in need. The shine didn't disappear. There had to be layers and layers of wax to muscle up the shine, and soft rubber heels seemed to cushion rather than scrape the finish.

Buffing was like working a weight loss vibrating machine. I was glad to have that job over some of the other tasks. One was hands-and-knees toothbrush cleaning the ornately designed chapel benches. Brush and scrub; brush and scrub! Another was dusting the antique furniture. I had one episode where I broke a two-foot-high decorated vase while slipping on a loose rug. Give me an open hallway, where my two feet had only to stay stable with the pulsating of the buffer machine! After all, I was building muscle, wasn't I?

The laundry room called on Lora and me again. She and I were assigned to the room-sized mangle, where we caught the hot, dry sheets as they came out and, in sync, made sure they got folded according to Sister Blanda's direction. The sheets rolled out continuously and were steaming. We moved fast: corners across, fold, corners up, fold, corners down, fold, and fold again. The greatest fault of the laundry room would be to let a sheet fall to the concrete floor. Once in a while, we took over the job of feeding the wet sheets into the mangle and let two others catch the hot sheets. I was glad we took showers on Saturday since the day's labor called for body refreshing.

Sister Blanda, the laundry supervisor, was one of the weirdest people I ever met. She called us young sisters "incubators." She had no sense of humor, gave directions in syllables rather than sentences, and offered no sympathy for the heat and steam coming at us from every direction. Despite my attempts to be friendly with her, she ignored me. "That's just Sister's way," my novice mistress would say. We were to get a job done so we could go on and do the next task. Weekly we mangled hundreds of sheets and then joined the others who were ironing our coifs, lightly starched to keep their shape. If I was lucky enough to miss the fussy job of coif ironing, I got to sort the clothes into their proper bins—a much less-hot job.

Each piece of clothing found its rightful bin as we matched number to bin. Months before I entered the convent, as would have been true of women before me, I received a package of numbers that I sewed onto my clothes. Numbers were recycled, but I was the first to get number 828; it meant at least 827 other Sisters had numbers before me. I always thought it was a successful day when every piece of clothing had a number. This rarely happened. Sometimes the thread from the stitching was still visible, but the number fell off. Sometimes there was no sign that a number had ever been there. We had an important lost-and-found box that held an honor system where items were able to be claimed. I couldn't imagine a Sister claiming anything not belonging to herself. Our target was to have laundry done by the noon meal, and I don't ever remember missing that deadline.

Another chore all novices were engaged in was working in the kitchen. I was first introduced to the multi-gallon potato-peeling machine. We'd load it with water and potatoes, and in a few minutes, with loud grinding and spurting, we'd have hundreds of peeled potatoes. I was relieved when assigned the final task of removing the remaining eyes rather than cleaning the peeling machine, which took longer than the tasks of filling the machine with potatoes and removing the eyes put together.

Loading the massive dishwasher was another select novice job. A routine which probably had been set decades before kept the task robotic—scrape, separate, soak, load, scrape, separate, soak, load. Hundreds of dishes got washed and dried rapidly.

Sisters Roy and Bertha Ann, along with apprentice Sister Thadine, who was just one year older than me, were our kitchen cooks. They would grumble over the spills and hesitancies we showed, especially when helping with the food, but somehow I always left the kitchen with a smile on my face. They had a spirit of service, and their meals were like gifts presented to the Sisters. Inspired by our cooks, I told Reverend Mother I'd like to be a cook rather than a teacher, but she must have filed that in the "forget that request" drawer since each semester I was assigned more studies and eventually was sent off to teach.

Three dishes they served brought me close to gagging. One was soft-boiled eggs, where the three-minute timer must have been broken since the eggs often came out raw and cold. A quick peek at our mistress was met with a "Don't you say anything. Just eat." Not much different than my mom's message of "Think of the poor children of China who don't have anything to eat."

The second dish was hash, which was made up of every leftover in the refrigerator. I don't mind hash; in fact, I like it, but somehow they seemed to make it when liver was leftover, and the hash became *liver hash*. Every other good meal mixed together for hash—meatloaf, chicken, potatoes, veggies—was lost to the taste of liver.

The third dish that made me gag, was talked about with much anticipation. It was a special dish served every Christmas Eve—oyster soup. Not ever having had oysters before and not liking them floating in the buttery broth, I choked. I couldn't imagine anyone looking forward to those slimy, slippery, gray creatures. One year I managed to sit next to someone who had told me she loved oyster soup; we were able to switch her empty bowl with my full bowl without anyone noticing.

Two of us at a time served as assistant sacristans. Sister Agnes, chief sacristan, was pure business, and it was serious. I learned never to walk from point A to point B without carrying something—we weren't to waste time moving empty-handed. There were many doors to open, and she taught us to lock and unlock doors efficiently: turn to the left to unlock; turn to the right to lock. A light was to be turned off as soon as we didn't need it; we were never to leave a room with a light left on.

Perhaps it was the German roots of the Sisters of Saint Francis of Mary Immaculate that made time and efficiencies highly valued. Perfection was expected.

I learned greater perfection especially when I assisted the general secretary, Sister Mary of the Angels, with typing and filing. In the era of typewriters and ineffective correction tools, I couldn't make mistakes. I was both scared and proud to be selected for such a trusted position. That office held the congregation's secrets, and I couldn't talk about anything I read or we did there. Of course, we did little talking in the Novitiate anyway, so I wasn't challenged much to be silent.

Hardly a chore, I loved Sunday morning choir practice when both years of novices as well as the postulants attended. From nine to noon each Sunday, we met in the auditorium with Sister Raphael to practice singing. *Do, re, mi, fa, so, la, ti, do. La, la, la, lou, lou, lou, ah, uh, oh, eh, ih*…exercise after exercise. Sister Raphael would stand in front and direct the vocal exercises until my mouth couldn't shape another syllable. Then the serious practice would begin. Song after song was rehearsed again and again. I especially loved the

Latin hymns—the "Magnificat" and "Ave Maria." I couldn't really sing the high notes of a soprano and wasn't able to sing anything but melody, and then only if a strong voice was beside or behind me.

Choir practice during the early convent years as well as years in my high-school glee club freed me to sing my heart out in any group singing environment. I felt honored to be in the glee club since only a select group of students got chosen. I was confronted with the reality when I heard Sister Clarita say to someone as I walked by, "This one doesn't have a voice, but I chose her anyway since she won't get much in life."

The Doorbell

Whatever you do, you need courage. Whatever course you decide
upon, there is always someone to tell you that you are wrong.

—RALPH WALDO EMERSON

IT WAS TWO YEARS AFTER I entered the convent that my dad rang the
Motherhouse doorbell to take me home. Sister Cyrinus talked with him. Mom
was dying, Dad told her, and I had to come home immediately. I don't know
what else was said. Dad must have gone home angry and helpless, because he
got nowhere. I wasn't called to talk with him. Superior Generals must have
been used to dealing with such parents.

Mom wasn't dying, I knew. She had a hysterectomy and was sicker than
she had ever been. Dad was worried and for the first time was in charge of the
household and three young boys.

Before I entered, Dad had offered me a car, a home, anything I wanted
as long as I wouldn't "give my life away." In my teenage wisdom, mixed with
a stubbornness to make my own decisions, and with the inspiration of char-
ismatic high-school teachers, I knew I had a calling to serve God and others.
And to add to my motivation, I was entering to pray for the salvation of Dad's
soul since he had given up on God, church, or anything religious, especially
since the church took his only daughter.

When Mother Superior heard my story, she allowed me to stay, and from that day on, I didn't want to look at her for fear she'd change her mind and send me home.

I felt much angst over how I would respond to my dad.

JMJF
September 20, 1960
Dear Dad,

I've lost count as to how many times I've started this letter and started again. I want to sit down and talk with you the way we used to. Wouldn't it be nice if I could come home and come back again when I wanted to? But that isn't how it works, and all we can do is make the best of it. I would like to be home now more than ever. I know I could be giving you and Mom much help and yet as unexplainable as it seems, I know I am doing the right thing by staying here.

Although things are rough around the house, Dad, I bet you must admit the cooking gets finished (some way or other), the boys go to school and you go to work.

Dad, your note talks about my trip downtown and wishes I would have called you. I'll let you in on a secret—I didn't have a dime to call you and I'm sure, if I did, I wouldn't be sneaky about it. When I joined the convent, I decided to be the best I could and that means obeying rules. Would you want your daughter to be anything else?

With these little sermons, I'd probably be better as a priest, yes? I know you're not angry, Dad, only concerned. I hope I've explained something to you.

I'll be writing in a few weeks again, but until then be a good cook. Love to Mom and the boys.

Your loving daughter,
Nancy
Sister Victor Marie

Entertainment and Fun

‿ᴄ

Life is playfulness…we need to play
that we can rediscover the magical around us.

—Flora Colao

My letters home captured the simplicity of fun we had. I was content in just about everything I did; within and outside the convent walls was pleasing whether it was walking over the Center Street bridge to go to the doctor or having a summer barbeque near the storage room that held my trunk.

In the summer, Sister Edward and I were responsible for barbequing our evening meal. We'd set out the grill on the drive-through path between the laundry room and the trunk room. We took our job seriously and found ourselves in the laundry room after the grilling to scrub the grilling rack until it was shiny new. We had such a strong sense of service that missing the visiting everyone else was doing wasn't a deprivation but a joy. Having known Sister Edward, who was an Aspirant at our high school, I had a comfortable history with her. Aspirants were young girls who lived together away from their home in a convent-like atmosphere during their high-school years and went to school with regular high-school girls like myself.

In the recreation room, we played cards, usually canasta. Sister Anacleta loved canasta, and we learned who the winner would be that night; it was intuitively accepted that no one but our novice mistress would win.

We'd turned any loose sheet of wrapping paper or art supply into a project. Since gift giving was at a minimum, I learned regifting early on and how to add my personal touch by wrapping each gift with a creative flair.

My budding writing interests led me to write and direct a play on Francis and the Sultan, in which my classmates obligingly performed. For years after, Sister Fabian never failed to remind me of what I asked her to go through on those play-practicing days. From being *shy, tall, and helpful* as described of me in my eighth-grade yearbook, I was becoming outgoing, a producer, and a director. I felt confidence growing and was loving the me that was blossoming.

Postulants after a "wounded war" play battle

Advanced Chores

I slept and dreamt that life was joy. I awoke and saw that
life was service. I acted and behold, service was joy.

—*Rabindranath Tagore*

By second year Novitiate, when our laundry duties were handed off to
the first years, we were given more responsible chores like ringing the morning
bell, locking the convent doors at night, and working as nurses' aides at Our
Lady of Angels Retirement Home.

Directly across the hall from our chapel was an alcove that housed a set of
narrow stairs leading to the convent bell. The stairs reminded me of those in
a Hitchcock movie—short footed, winding, and dark. For over a century, the
Sisters carried the tradition of ringing the bell three times a day—five o'clock
wake up and for the Angelus at noon and again six o'clock. The cord was thick
and the bell was heavy and learning how to ring it was an art: for a total count
of eighteen—one, two, three, pause; one, two, three, pause.

It was only in the 1980s that neighbors requested that the bell go silent.
The bell ringing of the Angelus, a tradition recorded to have begun back in
the eleventh century, was to remind us of the Incarnation of Jesus.

In the 1960s, the bell was just part of convent life, and we found its ringing helpful not only for spiritual reflection but to ensure timely attendance at
events—we ate our main meal at noon, so no matter where I was on campus,

I could make it to my dining room on time. The same was true at six when the first sound of the bell reminded me to get to chapel where we said Vespers at six thirty.

Mine was a sleepless week when I was assigned to ring the early bell. Normally I could rise rather easily, but several novices had missed the 5:00 a.m. deadline. I feared I would be the next one. And I was! Imagine my surprise when I was awakened at 5:10 a.m. with someone else ringing the bell. I knelt for breakfast that next day as my penance.

Locking the convent doors, especially those at the bottom level of the Motherhouse, was scary. I was grateful that two of us were assigned. The corridors were dimly lit, and the shadows of the night crept through the glass-paneled doors. One never knew who might be there; we had a lot of beggars who stopped at the convent's kitchen doors. I hadn't met beggars before and feared for what I didn't know. I had them in the category of boogey-men and escaped prisoners, both of which filled my childhood nightmares. They were the men who'd come and get me if I didn't behave, my dad use to threaten.

The only creepy character I ever met walking the halls was a dead rat, a foot-long dead rat. It was early Saturday morning when I was alone downstairs, taking some last-minute clothes to the laundry. There he lay in the middle of the hall, the sun ray aimed right at his lifeless body. I looked to find help, but no one else was around and it was still grand silence. Should I run? Should I get help? I don't know where the adrenaline came from, but I found some newspaper, wrapped him up, and dropped him in the hallway garage can. I never told anyone. I knew garbage got emptied every day, so I didn't fear any consequences. None came.

Working at Our Lady of Angels as a nurses' aide was added to our schedule. Sister Peter, one of two nurses in the community and lead nurse at the retirement home, trained and supervised our activities. I was assigned the lay people's floor and was expected to know what to do and how to do it. One day I was asked to assist in a patient's shower. This patient stood as tall as me and exercised a fierce fight. She wasn't about to be helped. Her diminishing mind held no reason, and her size held much resistance. The last time I showered anyone was my baby brother Larry, whose splash from little legs brought delight. This woman's physical resistance overcame me, and I walked out of the shower room, in full habit, fully drenched. She just smiled. I think she knew what she was doing more than she appeared.

Early Vowed Years

1961–1964

Of everything else, we were women in love.

—Novitiate, the movie

The Juniorate

Whatever you can do or dream you can begin it.

—Goethe

Two years of the Novitiate ran quickly by, and with both Sisters Anacleta and Cyrinus's oversight, we were quite prepared to be temporary professed Sisters. That meant we made the vows of poverty, chastity, and obedience for one year in a three-year cycle, and we replaced the white veil with a black veil—a major step in becoming a full-fledged Sister because now we looked like one. We dressed our habit with a large crucifix that hung from a black cord.

Commitment of vows was part of the large ceremony held at the cathedral. Women, now younger than me, were receiving their habits for the first time. Women older than me were making their final vows. It felt comfortable to find myself among them. It was 1961, and the decade that was to shake up the church and the world had not yet exploded.

I, among eighteen remaining classmates, stepped forward. While I waited to begin my journey up the cathedral aisle, I noticed the silence of my soft-rubber nun shoes. I touched the ivory-colored rope that hung around my waist and draped into three knots—three knots that this day forward would have added meaning. I would pledge to live in poverty, chastity, and obedience.

Sister Anacleta, our novice mistress, had given many talks on the vows, preparing us for this day—what they were and how we'd be challenged to live them. Those talks seemed to have little emotional impact on me. I was then nineteen and basically lived them my entire life. Nothing much was changing except that I was publicly pledging the vows as a religious woman.

My growing-up years were coated in simple living—Dad took on labor-based jobs, which were rather sporadic at first; we lived without much; Mom didn't work but made my clothes (back when fabric and thread were cheap) and served a lot of hamburger meals, hamburger being the cheapest meat in town. I remember how thrilled Dad was to be able to get my brother Tom and me Schwinn bikes. Schwinn had introduced a new concept of locally run dealerships, and Dad was enamored by the concept. I would not be a bit surprise if he applied his growing negotiation skills to get a good price from the owner. It wasn't until he started building homes that our family sustained a comfortable income.

Besides material simplicity, the *spirit* of poverty was reinforced in high school by the Sisters and especially through the Saint Francis Club. That spirit was defined as not to cling to material belongings, friendships, or any element of life. "Letting go" was a common and encouraged practice.

I lived in chastity perhaps a bit due to my childlike mindset, but also out of fear of what my father would do if I didn't. The Sisters reinforced a chaste life when they, along with most of the Catholic church, condemned my teenage idol, Elvis Presley, for rolling and gyrating his hips. They insisted we attach two-inch straps to the era's popular strapless prom dresses. I remember quite anxiously returning to school after prom, confessing to Sister Margaret that George, my prom date, kissed me on the cheek. I feared I might have done something that elicited that level of affection.

One of the actions of The Sodality of Our Lady was to post sayings on the tile walls that reminded us to live chastely, especially near and around prom. Quotes from the Bible and popular saints were cited. One quotation was *Avoid immorality. Every other sin a person commits is outside the body, but the immoral person sins against his own body* from 1 Corinthians 6:18. Saint Maria Goretti was upheld strongly, and I have a hunch that's why my friend JoAnn chose her name when she became a novice.

To be obedient was the only way I knew how to live. Adults told me what to do, and for the most part, I did it. Fear mingled with the drive for perfection, and avoidance of shame stifled any "disobedience" I might have wanted to do. It didn't take much in those young years to adapt to the rules and regulations of the convent. I no longer was obeying out of fear of my dad's punishment but for a higher good—to serve God. It felt freeing. Nothing seemed to be over-controlling or *stupid*, as later my kids described rules I tried to enforce on them. Back then I obeyed because I wanted to live wholly and fully in God and was convinced that the rules put upon me would lead me to be a worthy Sister.

So, on that August day in 1961, I, Sister Victor Marie, pledged publicly to live in poverty, chastity, and obedience. My family came, and we celebrated again on the familiar campus grounds. More than anything, that day reinforced for my dad that I was serious about being a religious woman and intended to stay. He just shook his head; he didn't understand. As I look back on that day and the one that finalized my commitment three years later, I realize that my decisions were based more on the desire to live as I wished to live and not the way my dad had tried to define for me. I was cradled in a safe environment, loving the simplicity of life—so defined it was easy to know what to do. And I wanted a defined life. It wasn't until I was "on mission" that disillusionment and growing self-confidence began to challenge my commitment.

In past years professed Sisters were first sent out on mission, which, due to the reduced study schedule in the Novitiate, delayed college graduation. Many Sisters talked about the ten to twelve years it took them to get their bachelor's degrees. With teaching requirements getting more rigid, that practice forced a change. Our group was one of the first to stay home for another year, creating a fourth year at the Motherhouse.

I was getting anxious to teach; studying was becoming boring, but my classmates and I were in this situation together, and we made the most of it. I took seventeen hour credits each semester and had just six credit hours to finish at the end of the year when I was given my first teaching assignment.

A section of the Motherhouse had been renovated for "Juniors" to live in—it was at the south end of the building, above the Sisters' tutoring center and the classrooms the college used. We were closer to the auditorium, where we continued our Sunday morning choir practice. A narrow, circular set of stairs, right off the auditorium led to our fourth-floor dormitory. We were closer to the Three Oaks entrance, and I found myself still enjoying seeing a full image of myself in the full-length glass doors. If no one was around, I found myself spinning around just to see what the movement looked like.

Being a Sister meant more than praying, studying, and obeying rules, which were beginning to feel like controlling house rules with little meaning to life or to serving God. I was anxious to serve God in a bigger way, serve Him by *doing*, not just living a life of regulated *being*. One of our Sisters had just left our community to become a Poor Clare, a religious woman who lived in a monastery and spent her time in silence and prayer. I was happy for her, yet I knew that a more-cloistered life was definitely not for me.

During my junior year at the Motherhouse, I continued taking several journalism classes and was appointed to the college newspaper, the *Interlude*. I was listed as a newsletter staff member in the January 12, 1961, edition and had several articles published in the next couple years. I also published in the college magazine, *Piper's Papers*. Writing opened me to a different world. I now had recognized responsibility to a larger audience than the Sisters. Not only did I love being a Sister, but I loved being a writer. I almost had my bachelor's degree and was close to going on mission. I was thriving. I posted a few articles in this memoir.

Sister Francine, our Juniorate mistress, was an intelligent, scholarly woman who scared me. I had chosen not to study French because she taught it at the college. As I got to know her, I gained a great respect for her but did so slowly and gingerly.

After our first full year in the Juniorate, we were sent on mission and, until we made final vows, would return back to the Juniorate in the summer. In my first summer back, I brought with me expectations that didn't match what Sister Francine believed how a junior Sister should conduct herself.

I had assumed being the chairperson of the Young Christian Students (YCS) Movement general conference at Notre Dame University and had multiple contacts to make to get the conference organized. I knew I had to ask permission to use a phone but didn't expect the answer I got. No!

Junior Sisters didn't use a Motherhouse phone—ever! It took multiple conversations between us before I finally got permission to not only use the phone but also not have to ask her permission every time I needed to make a call. Once I convinced her I wasn't going to make unnecessary calls and had a job to do, Sister Francine proved to be reasonable and generous.

As did the other mistresses, she offered weekly talks on Franciscan spirituality. I cherished her talks. Although she was a French teacher, she could have been a theologian; her lectures were both inspiring and practical. I felt filled with joy when I listened to her. I have a hunch my attitude changed more positively toward her once she and I formed a mutual and more adult-like relationship.

A frequent theme of her talks was on the integrity of our spiritual life as we begin our life of mission and service. She spoke of the tension we would feel—pulled into an active life where dedication to serving would challenge us to set aside our first calling, to be religious women, women of God, for God and with God. They were motivating and inspiring words. Truly I knew I would always be first a vowed woman to my God. It only took my first mission assignment to understand how difficult keeping my life focused on my spiritual life would become.

As Junior Sisters we sang at a Mass at Stateville Penitentiary in Joliet, IL. Pictured is our class with accompanying priests, musicians and superiors. Sister Francine is kneeling in second row farthest left; Sister Raphael, our choir director is to her right and Sister Zita is above Sister Raphael. I am standing, upper row, second from the right.

Preparing to Go on Mission

Service to others is the rent you pay for your room here on earth.

—MUHAMMED ALI

BEING SENT TO SERVE AT a specific parish or organization, all sponsored by the congregation, was a major step in a young Sister's life. I could hardly wait and was excited to be attending my first missioning ceremony.

Receiving notice was not a small ritual and reminded me of the sacredness the convent placed on silence. We assembled in the auditorium. Silence! Each Sister's name was read one at a time, oldest to youngest. Each stepped forth, received an envelope from Reverend Mother, and returned to her seat. Silence! I thought I heard a gasp several times. The next Sister was already on her way up. Our group's names finally began being called. We were called in rank according to our age: "Sister Eric, Sister Georgia, Sister Margarita, Sister Regine, Sister Maria Goretti, Sister Mary Benedicta [I gulped and got ready], Sister Victor Marie, Sister Melanie…." Silence. Prayer and a song, and we went to bed. It wasn't until Grand Silence was broken the next morning that we could share. I wonder now if there was any passing around of notes between more seasoned Sisters. I know I wouldn't have thought to disobey back then. In turn, I felt numb—I didn't know enough to feel or do anything else.

I was being sent to teach fourth grade at Saint Pascal's. I discovered that no one else in my group was going there. No one knew anyone who was missioned at Saint Pascal. No one was going to any parish close to mine. Some were headed to Ohio. Were they all going to be old Sisters and me? I had an adventure ahead of me. I was on my own.

We received our mission in mid-August and had two weeks to pack and get ready. It was a whirlwind. My trunk hadn't moved in five years; it still sat in the storage attic across from the laundry room, just where my parents had dropped it off. I had put things in and taken things out through the years, but I didn't own much and wasn't worried about not having enough space. My five-inch circular mirror was still with me, and I found myself packing that. Sister Benedicta was a saver and her trunk sat right next to mine; she struggled to get things arranged.

I knew about savers. I had been sent out to the attic to clean out the trunk of a Sister who had recently died. Part of our respectful ritual was to ensure that anything she had of value would find a proper home. This Sister had ten unused black cotton slips, a dozen cotton hose, something we hadn't been using for years, and multiple duplicate toiletries, one which had burst due to the unheated attic and possible length of time it was there. Hoarding for some of the Sisters, I was told, was an emotional reaction left from the 1929 Depression when families lost everything. Keeping more than I needed was so un-Franciscan in my mind. I struggled to understand why, even having lived through the Depression, a Sister would save as she did.

I would go on to spend nine years "on mission," teaching grades four through eight and spending my last two years in religious life as a principal. Seven of those years were to be in the inner city.

St. Pascal walkway.
Photo by Sr. Marianne Saieg

Final and Permanent Vows

Motivation is what gets you started.
Commitment is what keeps you going.

—Jim Rohn

Fifty years had passed when I found a tiny clear plastic box, the remnants of my final profession. Somehow it found its way to the bottom of my trunk, separated from everything else. I almost missed it when piling back travel books and other memorabilia that I didn't want to look at now.

My convent ring! A simple gold band with two engraved arrows pointing at the word *Jesus*. I knew without trying it on that it wouldn't fit. Although my weight had not changed since the 1960s, my fingers had grown thicker, and my ring size had increased by two sizes. I slipped it on my baby finger—just a little too big. *That's OK*, I said to myself. *It isn't supposed to fit.*

But on August 12, 1966, it fit. Unlike the many other times I walked from the Motherhouse in procession to the cathedral, this time was the big one. I was dedicating my life—forever—to be a woman of God as a Sister of Saint Francis of Mary Immaculate. My vows had been tested more than I thought they would. Being on mission thrust me into the rush of responsibility. I didn't have or perhaps didn't *take* the time to pray and focus on my relationship with God as much as I had in my early formation years. I was focused on others and my service. The latter seemed to minimize the prior, something I realized later couldn't be done in a marriage.

The sun shone as it always did on Profession Day, the warmth reminding me that under the wool habit and layers of head gear lived a woman warm in love and contentment.

The lines of women dedicating themselves to God were long. We were finally first; our class processed in front of the white-veil novices making first profession, in front of the postulants dressed as brides becoming novices, and in front of the congregation's administration. From the twenty-nine women who had walked up the 520 steps in 1958 to begin a life together, fifteen had completed the journey with me. Two others joined us since they waited an extra year to make profession.

I was twenty-five and had my bachelor's degree in English and three minors: journalism, education, and theology. I had been teaching for four years and loved being "on mission." I didn't like some of the behaviors of the Sisters I met on mission; they didn't have the charisma I had known of my teachers in high school. But I wasn't pledging to be like them; I was giving my life to be of service.

I was fully committed to religious life. My dad kept offering me reasons to come home and be with the family, and I kept assuring him that I was where I needed to be.

Final Profession gathering. Aunt Theresa (far left), loads of cousins, Dad in the middle, Uncle Arnie and Aunt Irma, Mom in the pretty white hat, brothers Bill and Larry standing to the right with Sr. Lucretia and me.

Mission Life

1963–1971

The best way to lose yourself is in the service of others.

—Mahatma Gandhi

Saint Pascal

1962-1964

MY FIRST TWO YEARS ON mission were at Saint Pascal, a middle-class community on the north side of Chicago—one of its oldest parishes, home parish of our late Cardinal George, whose fame is that he has been the only head of the diocese born and raised in the diocese.

Saint Pascal was blocks away from Dunning, a mental institution, and it was common to find a frequent visitor, one female patient, standing in the middle of our yard, talking to herself. We were trained to call the institution, and they would, without incident, guide her gently home.

Our yard, not fully enclosed, was a Spanish-designed courtyard with an arched walkway that led directly from the convent to the school. I can understand the attraction to wander there; it felt like solemn ground.

Saint Pascal School was relatively modern and hosted flat table desks with open slots for books, far different from the anchored down, flip-top wooden desks of my grammar school years at Saint John the Baptist in Joliet. I had fifty-four fourth graders nestled tightly in what could have been a large classroom had it only twenty students. They were well-disciplined and showed enough independence that I didn't feel overwhelmed and enough eagerness to learn that I wanted to give them my best.

I showed bubbly enthusiasm and was soon recognized as an effective teacher, one who was tapped to teach other teachers. That felt rewarding, except the chosen topic to teach was phonics. I hadn't learned phonics; I didn't know the difference between a short *a* and a long *a*, nor could I easily hear the difference in the sounds. I had learned to read through what was called *sight reading*, and I found it handicapping when faced with new words, even after giving workshops on reading and phonics. I remember later when the word "entrepreneur" was reintroduced into business language in the 1980s. I would practice and practice its pronunciation until I had it in memory.

Although most of the Sisters were older, I felt warmly accepted at Saint Pascal. I cherished my time with Sister Secunda, who, close to her retirement years, reminded me of my deceased Grandma Sophie, a robust, warm, and friendly soul who always had a kind word. I would spend years later visiting her at Our Lady of Angels Retirement Home. I have two paintings of hers that she gave me in her later life. She taught me a lot about aging: "My day," she shared, "is spent only doing the things I took for granted—dressing, bathing, praying, eating and sleeping."

The only other young Sister was Sister Suzanne. We had some fun kitchen time. One day close to Thanksgiving, we decided to make pie crusts, industry style. Having a recipe from the Motherhouse, we kneaded and rolled out twelve pie crusts, put wax paper between each, and layered them in the bottom of the freezer for future use. We discovered when we started to use them, that *kneading* pie crust dough only made the crusts tough; we lost all the flakiness of a tasty crust in our over-ambition. Now called Sister Joanne, she reminds me to this day that our pie baking improved, and we made many batches of pies to give away.

During my years at Saint Pascal, I started a branch of the Young Christian Students (YCS) with our seventh- and eighth-grade students. YCS was a movement to build social-minded youth leaders. It adopted the motto See, judge, act, from its mother organization, the Christian Family Movement (CFM) and was an empowering tool to stimulate social justice among young people. One of our junior-high students and quite a leader in her own right was a seventh-grader, Meg Guider. Meg helped me organize her classmates into a very active YCS group, and we spent many hours hosting meetings and going to local regional meetings to expand YCS's mission. Later Meg became our congregation's first associate and then entered the community, where today she continues to show her leadership capacity as a theology professor at Boston College.

YCS introduced me to other bright and dynamic educators and took me to different conferences in different parts of the country. I served as secretary to the organization and later as national director, each role strengthening my confidence in providing meaningful service both to my students and the larger Catholic community.

Mission life was directed by the superior, often not only the head mistress of the house but the school's principal. That was true at Saint Pascal with Sister Josine. Each mission was largely formed by the interpretation of the superior, many of whom were set in pre-Vatican traditions they knew best. Silence on mission was minimized due to professional responsibilities, but other restrictions remained. Sisters had no money, so attendance at any event was controlled by the superior.

When we heard that *Lawrence of Arabia* was showing at a local theater, we wanted to go. The theater was a few miles east of us, and it would mean taking a bus and walking a few blocks to get to the theater. Sister Josine questioned where the money would come from, and one Sister reminded her of the petty cash container that had built up from students paying fines for late books and other penalties. She gave each of us exact change—enough for the two-way bus trip and the show. There were lots of pennies, and since she gave us our money according to convent rank and I was the youngest, I received almost all my allotted money in pennies. I was nervous managing all that change, knowing that one penny lost meant no ride home. Arriving at the theater and paying for the show went well, but somehow, when sitting down in the dark theater, a few pennies slid out of my pocket. I found myself crawling on the sticky floor, habit and all, looking for every penny dropped. I found them all and spent the first part of the movie wiping off the goo the pennies had attracted. I only fully relaxed when the last penny went into the bus's money slot and I was safely on my way home.

Presenting at a YCS workshop

YCS Leadership Team. I don't remember the team members' names. I am the tallest in the back row.

Saint Boniface

1964-1967

AFTER TWO YEARS AT SAINT Pascal, I found myself restless. The congregation was opening a school in Goiana, Brazil, and I wanted to join the team. I dreamed of being a missionary. It didn't happen. Instead Reverend Mother Borromeo sent me to my first inner-city school, Saint Boniface, to teach sixth grade. Since she had been my principal for my first two years in high school, I wondered if she thought the shy, insecure girl she knew then wasn't up to the task of foreign mission work.

Unlike Saint Pascal with its lush green yards and well-kept streets and homes, Saint Boniface was close to the Chicago Loop, barren, with transition owning the space and tension spilling into the atmosphere.

My students were Puerto Rican, and their worth was measured by how dark their skin was. The lighter the skin and the less kinky the hair, the more highly they ranked themselves. Dark-black Puerto Ricans were at the lowest cultural status.

My students were poor. Their academic success was poorer. English, for many, was a second language, hardly learned. I became the upper-grade math teacher, and although I was always weak in math, I was successful because my students were below level. I could teach eighth graders fifth-grade math they hadn't yet mastered and did all right.

Saint Boniface turned out to be a joyous and growth-rendering experience. I felt nurtured and loved by my superior and principal, Sister Annarita, more than anyone in my life. She empowered latent talents in me. I learned to drive and was the designated driver for most errands. I was called on to use all the artistic talent I never knew I had—I taught art; I led the school choir yet hardly could hold a note. I used every technique that I had learned in my art classes from Sister Veronica and five years of Sunday choir practice from Sister Raphael.

I no longer got commendation solely from the outside with my YCS work. I found myself blossoming in confidence within the community. That is, until one Sister didn't like the attention I was getting.

In our convent home, it was obvious that our superior spent lots of time with me. I became her personal driver, I helped her with special projects, and I was assigned prime projects. I was a visible presence of her favor.

One Sister stopped talking *to* me and spent time talking *about* me. I tried to apologize, not sure what I had done but wanting the tension to stop. It didn't. I wept and asked for help when the congregation's assigned counselor, Sister Lizette, came for her yearly visit. Sister's words softened my victimized heart: "Sister, she is hurting. Feel sorry for her. She is not trying to hurt you." The words were soothing and opened my eyes. I was getting all the attention from our superior and principal; surely that Sister needed some attention too. I tried to avoid Sister Annarita when I could so as not to prompt the issues that Sister was having, but my need to be of service remained. Our relationship didn't improve much, and as I look back, I am sure my own needs to be loved and appreciated triggered some of the tension.

My commitment to be "of service" nagged another of the Sisters, one a year older than me, Sister Kieran. "For God's sake, Sister," she said, after I had just offered to do something. Walking up the stairs to the second floor of the convent, she yelled, "Why don't you let any of us do things around the house? How about letting us do something for you once in a while?" Oh my! Of course, I was selfishly giving and giving, not receiving and not letting others give and receive as they needed to do. That encounter left a major impact on me. How much I learned that selfless giving could be selfish receiving. How much I learned that others had giving needs besides me. I have been forever grateful.

I journaled and set it in my prayer book:

How have I today built up community?
R—respect—see whole mystery of a person—"look again"

E—encounter—really listen to others...and to God
C—concern—be interested, don't cast aside their ideas, problems
Watch for too much monologue, preconceived judgment utilitarianism in
my actions.

I found another older Sister at Saint Boniface, Sister Lucretia, who I emotionally adopted. Sister Lucretia had what I discovered was a behavior of several Sisters to get what she or the convent needed: asking for and receiving service, gifts, and attention from parishioners. She was not shy to ask for a ride or a donation, and she got it. I admired her bravery and her loyalty to congregational needs, although I couldn't do the same.

Seminars for inner-city teachers were spreading across the diocese, and I began to attend. It was there that I learned of the cultural tensions, not only between ethnic races but within them. Although I never taught in an African American school, I attended many "black is beautiful" seminars, taught by bright and articulate African Americans. "You are to blame for our fate. *You!*" First I was stunned. Then angry. How could I be accused? I found myself looking at myself, outside in. Dressed in full habit, having dedicated myself to God to serve others, I was being blamed for the African Americans' fate in life. Slavery? Come on! Depressed lives? Really! But I didn't stop going to the seminars; I needed and wanted to know more. It didn't take me long to understand the universal messages we were receiving—white privilege was present even among those of us who tried to separate from the prejudices and biases of the world. I had a lot to learn and accept—to support and encourage.

It was at Saint Boniface that my brother Tom came to visit with his bride-to-be and, on the side, said, "I hope you like her. If you don't, it's too bad, because I am going to marry her." I did like her and was deeply saddened when, eighteen years and five children later, they divorced. I sought permission to attend their wedding and was able to go to the ceremony but not their reception. Permissions were starting to open up, but, as I was told, convent practices were *slow* to change; attending a family member's wedding reception was not allowed. No one knew in 1965 how wrong the phrase "slow to change" was. In just a short few years, convent practices changed *fast*, leaving a spiral of swinging doors, empty classrooms, and mission confusion, challenging every practice and tradition that had defined us for centuries.

During this time, popularity of the Singing Nun, a Belgian Dominican songwriter, had swept the country. "Dominique" was high on the record charts. People told me I looked and acted like her and wondered if I played the guitar. I'd laugh, of course, and then, as interest in her music grew, I realized what a ministry she had, entertaining others. Maybe I *could* learn the guitar, I said to myself. Guitar was a popular instrument at our YCS gatherings due to Peter, Paul, and Mary's music, so I'd have lots of opportunity to use a newfound skill. And my confidence in my music ability had improved since leading the children's choir. My brother Bill, who was just launching what turned out to be a long career of guitar playing, lent me a guitar. Strum, strum, and strum. I memorized simple songs like "Beautiful Brown Eyes" and "She'll Be Coming Around the Mountain" and practiced and practiced; I found "Dominique" too difficult. With raw and sore fingers a few months later, I realized that I couldn't tell when the guitar was tuned nor whether I was on tune. I knew I wouldn't turn out to be the American version of the Singing Nun, but I could offer warm smiles like she did. I gave the guitar back to my brother. And I didn't consider competing with the *Flying Nun* that Sally Field, in the movie of the same name, portrayed a couple years later.

The younger sisters at St. Boniface enjoying a summer day. I am in the far right back.

Our Lady of Guadalupe

1967–1968

AFTER THREE YEARS OF SAINT Boniface, I found myself going to teach eighth grade in an all-Mexican school nestled on the far south side. A well-established Mexican parish and school run by the Claretian priests begun in 1947 was 100 percent Mexican; children from surrounding areas were bused to the school. Children of the neighborhood, all African American, went to other schools.

The school was just miles away from the steel mills that employed many south-siders. The steel mills were a leading economic sector, and immigrants found their way there. We learned to keep our windows shut since a light film of steel dust would creep within hours onto open window sills. A rotten egg odor was common. Somehow I adjusted to those discomforts since I knew my dad had worked at a steel plant during my youngest years. Fearing possible lung damage, I was grateful he was out of the steel business.

Our Lady of Guadalupe had no young Sisters. Rumor had it that Sisters whose style had not been met well in white middle-class parishes were sent to places like Our Lady of Guadalupe. The parents were more respectful of Sisters, no matter what they did.

Several of the Sisters spent recreation time expressing frustration over the *dumb* Mexicans and how wasteful learning was on them. One day an elderly, rather cranky Sister took her cane and pushed a second-grader up against a tree and said, "Go back where you belong." I was horrified.

It seemed through my idealistic eyes that the superior/principal could not control the disgruntled Sisters and the apparent racism. Mother Borromeo was still in office, and I wrote her describing the situation. I turned my shock and embarrassment to arrogance, I'm sure. I heard nothing back. The next August I was the only one who got transferred.

My experience at Our Lady of Guadalupe made me shockingly aware that racism had infiltrated the convent, and I was not surprise when two years later, Sister Jeanne, who was working in the black community of Englewood, and myself were asked to prepare community-wide workshops to combat antiquated thinking. Today our Sisters are leaders in the antiracism movement.

While at Our Lady of Guadalupe, I took public speaking classes from the Gabriel Richard Institute. "I can't lose. Why? I've got faith, courage, and *enTHUSiasm*," accenting the second syllable of enthusiasm, we would chant week after week, taking turns giving talks and being critiqued. I can credit Gabriel Richard for turning a rather reluctant speaker into a confident one, skills that would support me the rest of my professional life.

1st Communicant posing with me in front of a bulletin board I created.

My 8th graders performing for a Mexican holiday.

Saint Ludmilla

1968–1969

I APPROACHED MY NEW PARISH disillusioned by the experience at Our Lady of Guadalupe. Quickly I found out it was different there. For one thing, we had a young and easy-going principal, Sister Sylvia. One thing did *stink*: Blackie, our perpetual house guest.

An all-black Labrador retriever, Blackie had an unnamed disease which caused him to emit an overpowering odor, no matter the care he received. Sister Emma, our housekeeper, took great care of him. He was, after all, her constant companion when we were teaching. It didn't help that Blackie was friendly. Wagging his tail to welcome us seemed to emit a greater odor. If not in Sister Emma's room, he frequented the recreation room. My oversensitive smelling senses were challenged.

Saint Ludmilla, a parish built in the 1890s, was in the area of the city called Little Village and was in transition, with about one-half Czech and one-half Mexican families. Unlike Saint Boniface, ripe with changing tensions, and Our Lady of Guadalupe, solidly Mexican, Saint Ludmilla seemed to be adjusting well to its new neighbors. I taught eighth grade and enjoyed it there. I was surprised to be transferred after only a year. I felt wanted and successful.

My time on mission, interacting with other Sisters, had its difficult times, yet Saint Ludmilla was different. It was a friendly family of professionals. I carry with me yet today friendship with Sister Odelia and remember fondly the times we shared together. On one occasion I needed help at an Iowa YCS conference and asked Sister Odelia to go with me. Hesitantly she questioned her ability. I assure her that she could do it, and she came with me, delightfully surprised at her proneness. Later she ventured far beyond Iowa to serve for many years in our Brazilian missions.

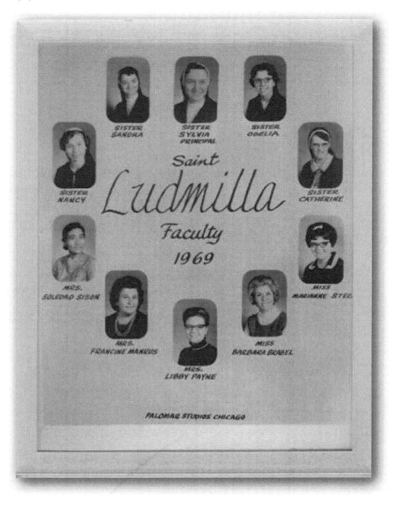

Saint Procopius

1969–1971

I LEFT LITTLE VILLAGE AND went to Pilsen, just a few miles east of Saint Ludmilla and a few miles west of the Loop. Pilsen was a well-established Mexican community, receiving its first Mexican immigrants shortly after WWII. There were churches every few blocks—having been built by each ethnic group that found its way just miles west of the Loop—Italian, Bohemian, Polish and more. Pilsen itself is named after a city in Bohemia. Already in the late '60s they were becoming predominantly Hispanic.

At twenty-seven, I became the youngest principal the elementary school had ever had and probably the most unprepared. I was going through doubts about my religious vocation. I felt changes in my heart, loneliness, and a sense of being unfulfilled, having moved from inner-city to inner-city parish and living mainly with middle-aged, crabby Sisters who seemed to just be putting in time. Having lived in nine homes before I turned seventeen should have prepared me for my frequent convent homes, but it didn't.

Yet, the ministry was inviting, and the opportunity to be responsible for the school was enticing. I set aside my emotions and plunged into my work.

Unlike other Hispanic communities I served, Pilsen was well established. It had cultural advantage, having its Mexican culture well established in the community. The people were proud of their heritage; stores and lifestyle were well defined. They, like Saint Boniface Puerto Rican families, had their class-status rankings. Mexicans directly from Mexico were imported for low-level restaurant work and lived in basements, cot-to-cot. Mexicans from Texas,

"Tex-Mexs," were considered only half Mexican, and Chicago-born Mexicans ruled, gang-like style.

Many of the Chicago-born men were being recruited into the Latin Kings and the Satan Disciples, two rivaling gangs taking over the streets and businesses. I stayed off Eighteenth Street, especially on Saturday nights when bullets flew freely over cars. These gangs still exist and have become more sophisticated with constitutions, manifestos, hierarchical structures, and international connections. Grandparents and parents recruit their young, and being a gang member for many has become part of Pilsen's family culture.

Latin Queens were being recruited by the Latin Kings, and Saint Procopius High School dealt with the girls exploding with delight to be chosen as a queen while flashing the gang's black and gold colors. I was grateful that the gangs had not recruited elementary-school children, as least as far as I ever knew.

In the late 1960s, these gangs were taking root in the neighborhood, and while multiple efforts by the police and the church were made to eliminate the gangs, we failed. A young priest at Saint Procopius as well as the Eighteenth-Street Team, of which I was part, dedicated much energy toward the endangered teens. Unfortunately in the priest's efforts to win their favor and turn toward the church as a healthy parenting image, he distributed money allotted by the city for summer labor without expecting any labor. The boys took it to reinforce their budding drug businesses.

Despite the established Hispanic atmosphere of Eighteen Street, Saint Procopius was still run by former Polish parishioners who would return back to the neighborhood to attend Mass and take over the school gym to play Bingo. They would check out the neighborhood each week and make comments about non-blooming plants and growing clutter. They were loyal to their former parish and continued to serve on the finance committee and any other organizing committee needed. The Benedictine priests who ran the parish appreciated their continued generosity and did little to discourage the discordance.

My staff was supportive, and I had wonderful teachers with Sister Marilyn, my classmate, teaching first grade, Sister Rebecca in fourth grade, and Al Pollock in eighth.

Sister Mary, the high-school principal, and I shared a classroom that had been divided into two offices by a common wall.

I had been warned that Sister Rebecca had given the former principal a difficult time. I was determined to find the best in her and spent focused energy on complimenting her on every positive thing I caught her doing. It didn't take long for us to bond and really like each other. Eventually when we both left the community, we rented an apartment together. I even stood up for her wedding and named my first daughter after her.

Al, single and attractive, found his way to my office almost every day for a midday smoke. I looked forward to his visits and the attention it brought me. Our relationship didn't turn romantic, and although I think I could have given into it, Al was dedicated to his mother and his stamp collection.

At one gala event sponsored by Como Inn, one of the finest Italian restaurants in the city, I found myself sitting next to Al, and following a couple glasses of wine, I placed my hand on his thigh. My heart raced, and shame took over. I was feeling feelings that shouldn't belong to me. He was a gentleman, and we never talked about it, but I noticed he didn't stop in my office as frequently after that.

These steerings were troubling, and I began to question more what I was doing staying in the convent.

Alcohol flowed freely at any event the Como Inn owner hosted. Besides dinner engagements he would take us out on his boat in Lake Michigan. Although having a 7 and 7 or two at my aunts and uncles' weddings since I was ten, I didn't know my limits on drinking. But after my uncomfortable behavior at the restaurant, I remained on high alert.

The years at Saint Procopius challenged and tempted my vocation. I began feeling emotions that hardly needed to be protected before. I had felt firm in my vows of poverty, obedience, *and* chastity, and I didn't seek doors of temptation. Those doors seemed to be opening on their own accord. Becoming part of the Eighteenth-Street Team opened them wider.

During my time at Saint Procopius, my dad took over a used car dealership and proudly gave me my first car—a 1964 green Nash Rambler. I was surprised at the gift since it held no bribe for me to leave the convent. I made sure Dad knew the car was not really mine but the convent car, yet I had opportunity to drive it. It became a necessary means of transportation as I drove back and forth to the team's headquarters every weekend. In fear of what a city bus on Eighteenth Street would transport, I didn't take the bus.

I thrust myself into the ministry and became a frequent visitor in my Procopius families' homes. Most of the homes were overcrowded with extended family members living with them; many families lived above restaurants they owned or managed. I soon had to deal with another frequent visitor in their homes—cockroaches. It seemed to be so common for the families that they didn't acknowledge their presence. I would see them boldly crawling along the edge of window sills. I learned to sit at the edge of a sofa, believing they wouldn't creep out of the deep crevices. And when I'd get home, I would shake my coat and check my clothes. It didn't stop me from visiting the families—I grew to love the families deeply.

With my convent veil now mostly in my convent trunk, I sought hairstyling. It was the era of poufy hair. Hair didn't lie flat, nor was it twisted and turned by rollers. It got *ratted,* leaving the hair standing tall and full. It was hard to fix it without professional help. One of my school parents, a hair stylist, offered me a discount. I rarely washed my hair but succumbed to weekly visits, when my hair would get washed and re-ratted for the week. It was almost like wearing convent head coverings; all I had to do during the week was readjust renegaded hair that moved out of place while I slept.

It was during my time at Saint Procopius that the congregation asked me to join Sister Jeanne in a community-wide effort to give our Sisters their first community-sponsored diversity training seminar, targeted for delivery in the summer of 1969. Jeanne and I began by attending a week-long sensitivity training workshop in Saint Louis, Missouri. This was followed by attending Chicago-based workshops on black and Hispanic cultures, Jeanne present at the workshops focused on African American culture and I at the Hispanic. Although busy as a new principal and a new member of the Eighteenth-Street Team, I found this work highly complementary to what I needed to know for my mission work and very emotionally rewarding on what I needed to learn about myself.

Sensitivity training focused on getting in touch with one's feelings in the here and now. I didn't know how to do that. "Don't talk about what you thought; talk about what you are feeling—this minute," echoed the facilitator over and over. "Be present now in the present! The only thing that matters this week is this moment; we don't want stories of the past or dreams of the future—just this moment—you in this moment."

I was to go on and attend a couple more week-long workshops of a similar nature, one with the Eighteenth-Street Team, in the end totaling four hundred hours of *sensitivity*. Each presented me with opportunity to become more deeply in touch with Nancy. The intention was to be rid of the false self, the role-playing self, and purely approach life and ministry more spontaneously and freely. What these experiences did was allow me to name feelings more freely, to understand what I was feeling more openly, and to react more honestly—each to support me daily yet today.

Eighteenth-Street Team

I was born the day I thought:
What is? What was?
And What if?

--Suzy Kassem

During the last two years I spent in the convent, 1969–1971, I was part of the Eighteenth-Street Team of twenty diocesan priests and religious women from different communities.

Principal by day at Saint Procopius and team member by evenings and weekends at Saint Vitus, the team's center, I was often "in the field" ministering to the Hispanic community.

The Eighteenth-Street Team was the brain child of Father John Ring, who was running the Hispanic Ministry Office for the Chicago Diocese. The purpose of the team was to give ministerial attention to the needs of Pilsen and Little Village.

Being part of the team gave me a new way to look at life. Unlike the ministry of my community, where most of the Sisters working in the inner city were elderly, all of us on the team were in our late twenties, early thirties, all full of energy and enthusiasm for ministry—all too whose hormones had discovered latent needs. Soon after we connected, people began to pair off. Two couples eventually married, and another two found mates outside the team. We worked hard and played hard. Since I moved into Saint Vitus in our team's second year, I had remained distant from the mating activity. Besides Al Pollack, who was my eighth-grade teacher, I found myself attracted to team member Al Sanchez, but his eyes were on a beautiful blue-eyed blond, Claire, whom he later married.

I discovered Manhattans, which were the favored drink of the team, and they flowed freely. After my second, I told Charlie, one of diocesan priests on the team who was known for his Manhattan-making, "I'm feeling a bit dizzy." He said, "That's the idea." I had a lot to learn. We drank. We smoked. We danced. We sang. Teenage activity that had been unengaged for years became alive.

Bar hopping, especially Irish bars, became a popular activity, especially near and around Saint Patrick's Day. We'd celebrate for weeks in advance. Although I haven't one ounce of Irish in me, I could sing every popular Irish song with every stanza along with the rest of them.

And compounded by the years of ministry experience we brought, we offered a robust presence to Eighteenth Street.

Some of us came with knowledge of Spanish; I was one who didn't. And so after that first year, I, along with several other team members, was sent to Puerto Rico for an intensive six-week language immersion. During the weekdays we lived and attended classes on the campus of the University of Puerto Rico in Ponce, at the far southern tip of Puerto Rico. On the weekends we traveled to the hills and barrios of the country. The natives taught me how to predict rain by watching the clouds move over the mountains.

We found Puerto Rican Spanish was different than Mexican Spanish— they spoke faster and clipped off the endings of their words. Since I knew neither dialect, I thought it wouldn't make a difference.

When I was at the college, learning German had its challenges. I could read the language and learn the grammar but couldn't translate the sounds into understanding or speaking it. And so it was with Spanish. I brought home a deeper understanding of the Puerto Rican people, their land, and their culture, but not the spoken language. I had to trust the children to translate to their parents.

That didn't always work out. One time I asked a fifth-grader to bring his parents to the school so we could talk about his behavior. He brought his mother, and during the translation, she smiled, reached out to hold her son's hand, and said "Ah, mi dulce nino" (my sweet boy). I knew something had failed.

Another time a fifteen-year-old eighth grader, tall and muscular, was bullying his classmates. Both parents came to my office and sat down cautiously. The boy had been caring for his sickly mother and was in and out of school for years; it seemed they expected the worst. The young man and I had had some serious conversations about his actions; I had isolated him from others on several occasions, yet no changes had occurred. When I explained his behaviors in my broken Spanish, and they listened in their broken English, their reaction was severe. The mother cried. The father got up and started beating the boy—continuous attacks on the head and shoulders. The shame, which I was to understand, was a cultural handicap—especially hearing about his son's actions in a *Catholic* school and from a nun.

In both situations, I learned that working without full capacity to choose and use the words I would find appropriate limited my effectiveness.

Eighteen Street Team. Founder Father John Ring is in the back row, farthest left. I am in the middle of the back row.

Then To Now

Breathe! Let go! And remind yourself that this very moment is the only one you know you have for sure.

--Oprah Winfrey

The Culture and the 1960s

*You cannot step a foot into the literature of the 1960s without
being told how "creative," "idealistic" and "loving" it was.*

—Roger Kimball

WE DIDN'T WATCH MUCH TV in the convent. Our big treat of the week was
Lawrence Welk on Saturday night. Welk was Catholic, hired Catholics to
perform, and made sure each performance contained "good, clean, and playful fun." I grew to love watching the show and looked forward to them. I
didn't know that Welk would remain a vital memory, since my mother-in-
law, Mabel, was one of his girls. During his radio days in South Dakota, he
introduced the "Maids of Melody"—Mabel, her twin sister, Mary, and Dee,
a good friend of theirs.

I hadn't missed television, and although I have fond memories of my childhood TV shows—Howdy Doody, Roy Rogers and Dale Evans, Hopalong
Cassidy, and the Lone Ranger, followed by high-school favorites, Teresa
Brewer, Pat Boone, and Elvis Presley—I adjusted well to not watching the
screen.

I didn't know what TV addiction was until Thursday, November 22,
1963, when John Kennedy was shot. I was teaching fifth grade at Saint Pascal,
and Sister Josine, the principal, interrupted the classroom to announce the cri-
sis. The silence shouted. The shock and confusion that followed the rest of the

day hung in the air like a thick fog. Shot at 12:30 p.m.; died at 1:35 p.m.! All after-school events were canceled; we rushed home, surprised to see the TV on. It stayed on all weekend. School was canceled on Friday and Monday. Clip after clip flashed, repeating themselves as news does, and each time sending an impact larger than the first time. Our beloved president, a *Catholic* man, a vibrant, young, promising democrat—gone! John Fitzgerald Kennedy!

It was hardly over, the loss of our beloved president, when another shocking event happened five years later. The leader of the African American civil rights movement, Martin Luther King Jr., met the same fate—April 4, 1968, shot and killed on the balcony of a Memphis hotel. We watched and prayed and worried about the state of our country. The TV again stayed on. King's words echoed over and over: *Darkness cannot drive out darkness; only light can do that. Hate cannot drive out hate; only love can do that.* I felt numb…and scared; I was in the heart of the inner city then and teaching at Our Lady of Guadalupe on Chicago's far south side. Our convent, across the street from the school, was surrounded by homes owned by African Americans.

Nightly for two weeks I could see neighbors hauling TVs and large kitchen appliances into their homes. My only conclusion was that they joined the mayhem on Roosevelt Road, where stores were being looted. Fortunately riots didn't happen on the south side, and no one was hurt there. It was though a time of uncertainty and concern. And, for one who had been sensitized by "the Black blight," having attended session after session led by African Americans, I felt their pain and that of our country intensely. Many of those feelings have been rushing back as I see a repeat of the same tension between African Americans and policemen that happened fifty years ago, added now with a hate and fear of Muslims.

It was only months later when a second Kennedy was assassinated—Robert, right after his nomination to the presidency—June 5, 1968, at the Ambassador Hotel in Los Angeles. The country was frozen in fear.

Authority was being challenged abundantly in multiple ways, not only with the assassination of key public figures or even the rebellion against the Vietnam War but also as an offshoot of Vatican II. It appeared that Vatican II opened the windows, as has been often quoted, as well as the doors, to the locked chambers and the untouchable sanctuaries. Obedience to bureaucratic rules was challenged. Sacred rituals were changed, the Mass was no longer in Latin, confession was set aside, and women were stepping forth into more leadership positions. The church was being defined as the People of God, not a building or an institution; relationships were important; people, not church rules, were the focus. We began offering the *kiss of peace* at Mass. We began talking in church before Mass began. Movements like YCS called forth leadership from the young.

The adults in charge of YCS felt a new sense of freedom in the church. We sat in circles at retreat gatherings that were no longer silent; we'd hold hands and sing and sway to "Kumbaya," "If I Had a Hammer" and "Leaving on a Jet Plane." We'd have outdoor Masses on the Notre Dame campus. We felt united in a mission, and we were growing a new church for a new generation.

The convent was changing. We stopped needing a companion when traveling; we didn't need to ask permission to leave a room. We were second-guessing traditional ways of doing things. The older Sisters were threatened, with some becoming critical and judgmental of the younger Sister's energy toward change. It was harder to live together. Restlessness abounded.

The world of the '60s, the world of the church, the world of society was a turbulent, exciting time.

Changes in attitude leaped rather than creeped in me. From not questioning any rules and being cooperative with convent standards, I felt a rebellion within me, and it carried me into the Eighteenth-Street Team and out of the convent.

Vatican II and Religious Life

If things start happening, don't stew.
Just go right along and you'll start happening, too.

—Dr. Seuss

Like a wrecking ball carried by the power of a large machine, Vatican II crashed much that was held sacred in religious life. Shock, deviance, and anger ran alongside exhilaration and a spirit of freedom like two gangs at war, one for law and order and another for freedom and revolution.

Vatican II's message to priests and vowed men and women was to find ways to connect more with the laity—to modernize ourselves so we would become more relevant. Two obvious changes that took hold were modifying the habit and returning back to our baptismal names. These trends became optional for us, and the majority of us changed. Some religious communities kept their traditions and yet today a few remain in full habit.

Mother Borromeo was heard to say, when the topic of modifying the habit was raised, "We will *never* show our hair." Sisters would gather in clusters and raise questions and concerns. "How will people recognize us if we don't wear a habit? Nuns aren't nuns if they don't look like nuns." Other sisters, myself included, were secretly looking at Simplicity and Butterick pattern books, trying to figure out how to transform our long wool habits into skirts and jackets. It was an upsetting time. Obedience was often shadowed by loyalty to authority. Knowing the Superior General was against the changes created tension among the most loyal of sisters.

In 1968, Mother Borromeo's term was complete, and Sister Francine, my former Juniorate mistress, was elected as congregation president. She chose not to use the titles historically given to the elected leader. She remained Sister, not Reverend Mother, Mother Superior, or Superior General. This humble change prepared more sisters to embrace the challenges of a changing age in religious life.

During the change, sewing machines were on night and day. In true poverty, we tore apart our T-shaped brown wool robes, working around worn spots to create skirts and tops. Style wasn't important—a simple design based on cost-saving practices was.

I felt excited to don my newly crafted clothes and place a small veil on my head, similar to what I wore as a postulant. There was a sense of liberation to see my legs once again and not worry about tripping on the scapular that I hadn't tucked well enough when climbing stairs. It was a new look, and I considered it a fresh start in religious life; I wanted to demonstrate the best of Vatican II. I wasn't pleased though to have to fix my hair again.

By 1969, we could introduce color, wearing simple blouses and skirts with some jewelry. Wearing a crucifix or any external sign that we were religious women was fading. We were merging into the crowd, no longer using our habit as the distinguishing factor of our vowed life. We were called to demonstrate our vowed life through lifestyle and Christian behavior. Some of us were more prepared than others. The exodus from the convent was in full swing.

When I retook my baptismal name and changed into lay clothing, I was perpetually professed, a vowed-for-life religious woman. I had major out-of-community responsibilities in Young Christian Students (YCS) and the Eighteenth-Street Team. I was an elementary-school principal, and at the same time, I was beginning to wonder if serving God in religious life was the only and best way to be a woman of service.

A post-Vatican II retreat in 1967 where I took notes reflected the changing tone of being a religious woman, given its title: "Laywoman in the Church."

Go into the world. Live a life of grace; live a life of love. Christ came to show us His love. Love = active concern for life and growth of those to be loved. We are very fortunate to be a woman and in love. We work from the sanctuary of our homes. We are the Church. Let people know you love Christ. "She must love God." Really show it! Christ needs us to carry Him to one another. We're Christ to the world.

This message was followed by recommended action.

Action is to be based on prayer and study. If my prayer has nothing to do with daily life, it has nothing to do with life. The task of a Christian is "to transpose Christ into the stuff of our daily existence." Our action must be rooted in God. How can we help people become real? Love makes us real. Serve with graciousness.

Leaving the Convent

Don't cry because it's over.
Smile because it happened.

—Dr. Seuss

Every year when I was able to visit my family's home, Dad would take me for a ride in his red Ford pickup to show me the homes he had built in Crest Hill. He was proud to drive me up and down Alma Drive, a street named after Mom. And every year he would offer me one of his homes as a bribe to leave religious life. One time he didn't.

"Nancy," he volunteered, "I've finally gotten use to you being in the convent." Twelve years later! Stunned, I mumbled, "Thanks, Dad." And then there was silence. I was already having thoughts about leaving, and now Dad was accepting my vocation. My mind went racing. Layer after layer of emotional defenses ripped away. I didn't need to be stalwart anymore; I didn't need to prove myself. I didn't need to act happy. My sensitivity training was in full gear.

Off and on, I had found myself in the balcony of Saint Vitus for Saturday evening Mass. My hair sometimes in rollers, getting ready for our team's evening dinner and get-together. I was becoming ashamed of my spiritual superficiality. Was I faking my vows? Wearing the habit was optional, and I wore it seldom. In general, I was representing very little of what being a Sister was or at least had been.

In turn, I was coming to the resolve that serving God and being in the convent was not an equals sign. I could do one without the other.

Yet I had never quit anything but learning how to play the guitar. My dad had reinforced commitment in our family many times. But times were changing. Rumor had it that Sisters were lined up outside Sister Francine's door, asking for dispensation from vows.

The nagging thought of leaving hung like a wet sheet swinging in the air. It hit me once in a while; the smell was sweet, but it just hung there.

The next time I went home, my brother Bill was outside washing his car. He greeted me as he still does today, "How are you, Sis?"

I was silent, and from nowhere tears began to well. "I'm not happy anymore." The words and the tears rushed out.

"Why don't you leave?" His words so openly spoken were an invitation.

It felt scary to hear them aloud after several months of silent rummaging. "Maybe I should," I said.

"What's stopping you?" My little brother, who I had cradled in my arms for his first seven years, was asking the right question. Mom was sickly during Bill's young years, and I, a ten-year-old, had assumed the surrogate role of nurturer and caregiver, his second mom. Now he was reversing that role with loving concern.

And then there was nothing else to say. I went into the house, visited with my parents, and spoke about it no more.

I went back to Saint Vitus, where I was living, and symbolically put the simple little veil deeper into my trunk. I didn't look at it again, nor did I remember it was there until I began this memoir. I lifted it carefully out of its tiny niched place, feeling strange to still have it—a sacred remembrance of a long-ago past. My fingers ran the rim of the white band, now accented by a yellow halo, probably from aging hair oil that had rested there for over forty years. A four-prong hair clip rested at the back. Two bobby pins still anchored the sides. A small once-gold-toned safety pin held both ends of the veil, a securing so that the veil wouldn't fly in my face. I smiled and remembered.

The little prayer I said when putting on my first veil came back to me: *May this veil, my dearest Jesus, hide me from the world and ever remind me of my consecration to Thy love and service.* Its size and style no longer hid much, yet its presence reminded me of the consecrated vows I took so many years ago.

The veil looked lovingly handcrafted. Did I make my own, or was it made by one of our seasoned seamstresses? I couldn't remember. I wanted to put it on—just to see how I would look so many years later. Yet it felt like a violation of my marriage vows to do so. I simply held it, kissed it, and put it in a newly organized convent memory box along with my other convent treasures. This veil, along with the crucifix I had worn when in full habit, and a gold band ring, are the only physical evidence that I was a nun.

It took a few more weeks to make an appointment with Sister Francine and then another few weeks before I could see her. The resolve only heightened.

What was left to do was fill out paperwork to apply to Rome for dispensation from my vows. I had boarded an emotional train that was headed elsewhere.

Months went by, and finally I heard the papers were waiting in Chicago; I was to make an appointment to sign them. Timing was perfect; I was ending the academic year at Saint Procopius, the Eighteenth-Street Team was beginning to dissolve, and some members already had wedding plans.

I arrived minutes before my appointment and found myself in a small windowless, yellow, florescent waiting room with dull turn-of-the-century furniture. I wondered how symbolic it was for what I was leaving. I hardly sat down when the interior door opened and out walked my classmate and first-grade teacher, Marilyn Fearday. She carried a legal-size envelope and had a smile on her face. I didn't need to ask what she was doing there. I knew, and she knew. We hugged and said something weird like, "See ya." I walked into the office, signed the forms, and walked out. As I turned and stepped toward the door, the priest who processed the papers said, "I wish you well." I mumbled, "Thank you," and was gone. No one else was in the waiting room. I had a skip in my step and a lump in my throat. It was over. Thirteen years dedicated to religious life!

At thirty-one, I was beginning again. I didn't have a job. I had no money except a small stipend the congregation gave me. I was in debt since the congregation had put a policy in place just a few years before: any perpetually vowed Sister who takes classes beyond her bachelor's degree and then leaves the congregation was to pay the congregation back; I had several master credit hours from the University of Chicago.

And yet, as strongly as I felt thirteen years ago when I walked up the 520 steps, I knew I was doing what was right for me. I was a woman of service, and I would continue to be one—just not in the convent. The rest I trusted would fall in place.

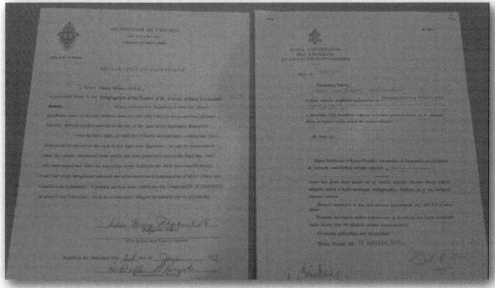

Dispensation from vows papers signed June 2, 1971

Entering the World

The thing that is really hard and really amazing, is giving up on being perfect and beginning the work of becoming yourself.

--ANNA QUINDLEN

THE 1960S HAD BEEN A vibrant, life-changing time for all America. The post-WWII prosperity and stable family life were upset by such events as the Vietnam War, the Black Power movement, the women's rights movement, and a myriad of other attitude changes. I wasn't fully in sync with all the attitudes and changes. I discovered that everyone *loved* the Beatles and that Beatles were not bugs, that weed was not a worthless plant to pull but one to smoke, and that bras could be burned instead of worn.

I discovered that people called hippies led the weed-smoking, bra-burning parties. They were the alternate thinkers of the era, running to Canada to avoid the draft, living in communes, dressing colorfully and freely. Although I had sung Peter, Paul, and Mary music at YCS youth rallies, I discovered hippies *embraced* their music and sought social justice while promoting a freer way of living, thinking, and believing.

When I left, I didn't become a hippie, but I admired them. I knew what it was like to step away from societal norms and be considered separate from the common mill of human folks. Hippies dressed uniquely; I had dressed uniquely at least during my early convent years. Hippies had a cause, and I had had a cause. Hippies stood out in a crowd, and so had I for years. I was ready though to become a common folk, whatever that meant. I knew I didn't want to be singled out.

I had absorbed the church-sponsored movements, especially Vatican II. I had a sense of the power growing in the African American community, among women who were finding their "identity" and fighting for equal rights, and a growing awareness of the gay community. Early on I could accept homosexuality, and I am glad, because in the early 1990s my oldest daughter announced she was a lesbian. And it was OK.

I was prepared to accept Mary Tyler Moore as my model over and above Margaret (a.k.a. Jane Wyatt) in the 1950s series *Father Knows Best*. It seems superficial to identify with TV characters, yet they were portraying the culture into which I thrust myself. I appreciated the laughter *All in the Family* and the *Carol Burnett Show* brought. I loved the escapism of *Charlie's Angels* and *Rockford Files*. I cherished the diversity and playfulness of life that each new-to-me TV show brought. I found out that colored televisions were the norm, and the twelve-inch screens I left in 1958 had doubled in size.

Adjustment to being part of the common folk wasn't easy. I discovered that I didn't know how to do small talk—to chat with people in ordinary conversations where the focus didn't come back to "What do you think, Sister?" or "We shouldn't talk about that with Sister here." I was feeling the insecurities of not knowing how to live without title, demonstrated respect, or expected authority. How are you? Tell me about your day? May I tell you about what happened? What do you think…? These weren't questions I found myself asking or even knowing to ask.

Our family conversations growing up had been minimal. Dad held firmly to the belief that children should be *seen and not heard*. I didn't learn how to chat. Convent talk was relegated to a one-hour recreation time, six or seven days a week. Most interaction exchanges were transactional—requests for permissions, directives to performance, confession toward forgiveness. With little practice in chatting in my early years, followed by significant silence in my early convent years, I knew I needed help.

When I began my master's degree in 1982, I asked a human-relations instructor to "teach me how to do small talk." I don't remember him offering me any words of wisdom, but eventually, as my comfort with myself met up with how casually people approached me, I became used to my new life.

It might have been an easier adjustment, had I realized how turbulent the world was and that my inner rumblings were just part of a societal pot. My uncertainties settled down a bit once I began teaching that fall. I found most of my colleagues at Saint Bonaventure to be ex-nuns, ex-seminarians, and ex-priests, so our common experiences helped build a sense of community, bringing comfort to being together.

I was living on the near north side of Chicago with the former Sister Rebecca, who had been my fourth-grade teacher at my final mission, Saint Procopius. She had left a year before and introduced me to the dating scene. She favored the bars, and I was OK with checking them out but quickly discovered that she'd leave me sitting alone once she got "picked up." I discovered that some women had "I'm sexy" written all over them; Becky was one of them. I wasn't.

Eventually I met a few guys and dated them briefly. One told me he chose me because he favored tall women; they were a better match for him. Although shorter than me, he said he had large parts to his body which did better with large women. I found out he wasn't looking for a relationship; he wanted a physical match. One quick date, and I didn't answer his calls after that. Another, a salesmen, confided after a couple dates that he was glad to meet me because he had read a book that teachers were great pick-ups. Dah! He added he was happily married, but given that he traveled so much, he wanted to know a few other women. Good-bye, buddy! My classmate Marilyn, who I had I met leaving the Vicar of Religious Office before me, introduced me to a policeman, a friend of her boyfriend. We dated a few times as couples, hung out at bars, and played pool. I dropped him when my date opened his car trunk to offer me treasures he had taken as bribes from south-side businesses. I'm outta here! I find it revealing that I don't remember what any of those men looked like or what their names were—a mere blur in my past.

Those months of undesirable dates added to my feelings of adjustment. It led me to a decision: I could remain single and happy without a man. It was soon after, at my new employment, Saint Bonaventure, that I met Harry, my future husband, a former seminarian.

My courtship with Harry wasn't as romantic as love stories often portray. We didn't send sweet little notes, sneak into a private closet when we were teaching at the same school, or have to be with each other every moment. He didn't give me flowers or surprise gifts. I didn't yearn for the next phone call. But it didn't take long to find we had a comfortable presence around each other.

It hadn't started out that way. He and I applied for the same job—Saint Bonaventure middle-grade coordinator in the start-up individualized learning program the Chicago diocese called IGE (individualized guided education). The principal, Diane Musial, a former sister herself, urged us to "talk it out." She assured us that we both could have jobs because there were other positions to fill in the school. I called Harry, and the conversation went something like this:

Me: *Hi, Harry, this is Nancy Polyak. Diane told me to call you and see if we could resolve which of us should take the grade four through six coordinator position. We both applied for the job. What are your thoughts?*
Harry: *Yes, Diane told me you'd be calling.*
Me: *Maybe we should look at who is more qualified.* (Wrong start, I later learned, because Harry is very competitive, and so am I.)
Harry: *It sounded like an interesting position, and it will be challenging.*
Me: *I just was an elementary-school principal, so I believe I have the administrative skills to run the program.* (Nothing like cutting right to the point.)
Silence. Another thing I learned later is that he is an introvert and has to think through his thoughts before answering.
Me: *Harry, are you there?*
Harry: *I think you should take it. I don't think I could work with you anyway.*
Ow! What do I say next?
Me: *You sure?*
Harry: *Yes, you take it. There is another job, teaching math in junior high. I'll take that one.*
Me: *OK. See you around. I'll tell Diane.*

I hung up, feeling shot down. I had called to get a resolution. We got one. But it didn't feel right. I set those feelings aside and called Diane. I got the job and left Harry to do his job; after all, he was going to teach in a whole other building. And after my uncomfortable experiences with men since I left the convent, I did not care what he thought. To close the story, I want to note that Harry claims he never said what I quoted.

By the middle of fall, school was in high gear and partying among faculty was easy. All of us gathered for lunch every day in the junior high building, often we'd go out for a drink after school, and it was common to hang out at someone's house for a weekend party. I was feeling comfortable since it was like repeating my social life with the Eighteenth-Street Team, now with no guilt, dispensed from my vows of poverty, chastity, and obedience. Harry and I didn't seek each other out but little by little got used to being in each other's presence.

Rather recently I asked him, among all the able-bodied colleagues on staff, why he invited me to help him with the political campaign of his friend running for office. "I liked you," he said, "and I needed help."

Even though I didn't know he had any feelings toward me, nor me to him, it felt natural "being around each other." We made a whirlwind night of it, hanging posters all over the north shore district, including climbing on a walkway across Lake Shore drive and dropping a large sign that said "Jim Houlihan for Illinois House of Representatives." (Jim was elected and has served Illinois in some elected capacity all his life.) As the sun rose, we finished our task, grabbed breakfast at a local greasy spoon, *Steak and Egger,* whose motto was "We doze but never close," went to my apartment for a quick nap—his six-foot-three frame hanging off my sofa and me in my cozy double bed. Tired but exhilarated with our successful night, we were dressed and off to a regular teaching day by eight o'clock.

This handsome, tall, thin, bearded man, two and a half years younger than me, bore a maturity I admired. He didn't make performance demands of me. For the most part, he didn't criticize, nor did he compliment. Once he told me the beige hot pants and brown leggings I wore to a party were a bit much. Harry was so unlike my father, who, while I was growing up, left no criticism unspoken, from attacking my face if I had a pimple to telling me to come in from the backyard while sunbathing in my swimsuit because I could invite trouble, slightly difficult to understand given that we had a tall fence surrounding our back yard.

For me, who was uncomfortable making small talk, I didn't feel we had to chat. And even though as time went on I became comfortable with my extroverted self and learned the art of chatting, I still cherish our silent times together.

Material things didn't matter to Harry. He lived simply. He was able to save money, even on a Catholic-school salary. He told me he had been saving to buy himself a Datsun 2-40Z, one of the "hottest" cars on the road, and instead invested in a town house. He was a dreamer with a responsible heart. I liked that.

I admired his commitment to social justice, values, and action, which have remained with him. I liked the robust and cultured gentleness that he emitted. So unlike my father, I became more and more attracted to him.

We began to see each other frequently and, in the fall of our second year, decided to get married. Even that wasn't romantic, as engagements go today. We had broken up when I asked him if he'd consider marrying me; he said no without much explanation. I was ready to start a family and knew, as hard as it was, that I had to move on if he didn't want me. A week after our break-up, he asked me to do one last thing: go to a baptism with him—by then his friends were used to having me around. Sitting on a sofa in his Downers Grove town house afterward, he began the conversation about us, and I could tell it came from much mental rehearsing.

He apologized for dismissing me and said he was just trying to protect himself. He was afraid. Tears silently began, and he didn't try to wipe them as he said he hadn't slept much. He wondered if I would still consider marrying him. He didn't get on his knee; he didn't have a ring. He offered me a warm and gentle heart, one that said he wanted to be with me.

When it came time to buy an engagement ring, we were both content with getting a ring with a pearl instead of a traditional diamond. It was August, just before beginning our second year at Saint Bonaventure. We decided to marry in spring of 1973. My dad's comment was, "He seems to be a nice guy, but he has to shave his beard before the wedding." Harry didn't and went on to wear a beard for many years into our marriage.

Mom, who had waited for her only daughter to be thirty-three to get married, said, "Why wait so long?" We moved our date back and married February 10, 1973. I asked mom if she still had her wedding dress. She told me she had taken it off and put it in a box and hadn't looked at it again. I loved the symbolism it brought as well as its simplicity of style; we decided to get it cleaned and ready for a second wearing.

That winter day was a crisp, cold, but sunny day when I sentimentally dressed in my mom's wedding gown, as later did my daughter, Terri, when she got married. A simple but lovely lightly ivoried white satin gown, Mom spent $12 for it in 1940; I spent $150 to add length and new lace in 1973, and in 2000, Terri spent $500 to eliminate the puffy sleeves and further modernize it. I believe it could uphold another wedding, maybe even in twenty years.

That day, I was again in Joliet in noisy white pumps and a simple wedding gown, not at the cathedral committing to be a bride of Christ but at my home parish, Saint John the Baptist, the parish where I made my childhood sacraments, went to school, and was introduced to the Joliet Franciscans. I didn't need to exercise custody of the eyes. I look around and was filled with joy as family and friends filled the church, including some Sister friends.

I was content. I was happy. This was where I needed to be. The time was right in 1958 to join a community where I learned what it meant to be a grown-up, loving and serving others. The time was right in 1973 to begin anew, partnering through life with the man I grew to love.

I became Mrs. Harry Davis. Throughout our marriage my in-laws and I had a never-spoken agreement that I, like his other friends, would call my husband Harry, but they would call him Harold in honor of his namesake uncle, Harold Lowell. It was one of the few differences we shared, and I felt blessed to have married into his family.

I went on to be a woman of service as I felt called. I taught at Saint Bonaventure and then, as a young mom, dabbled with part-time jobs including starting a catering service, proof reading for a publisher, and being the youth minister at our parish, Saint Cletus in LaGrange. These enterprises were replaced with full-time work teaching high school, then undergraduate school, followed by graduate school as a professor and administrator. In between I got a few degrees. In the middle eighties I began work in change management, first at the University of Illinois and then for a private consulting firm. In 1990, I opened my own consulting firm, Consulting Dynamics, Inc., and consulted in both corporate and church settings for twenty-five years.

I believe I am now in full retirement, after four attempts to retire. My final position was interim director of associates for the same congregation that I left, the Sisters of Saint Francis of Mary Immaculate.

Perhaps one's life doesn't go full circle, as some claim, but truly mine has come close. As a young woman in 1958, I stepped up those fourteen concrete steps of 520 Plainfield Road to become a Sister of Saint Francis of Mary Immaculate. I left in 1971. In middle age, 1984, when becoming a youth minister, I reconnected with the congregation as an associate, a lay person recommitting myself to Franciscan and Clarean values. And now in my senior years, I feel vitally connected to over 150 other associates, women and men, my husband being one of them, who identify with the Sister's mission and vision. I visit with the retired Sisters at Our Lady of Angels Retirement Home, some of whom I lived with and others I've known all my life; a few remain living who taught me. Being an associate has reinforced my life as a dedicated woman of service and prayer.

As I end, I tuck this memoir into my trunk, to lie side by side with all the memorabilia that allowed these thoughts to come alive within me.

Ever with my trunk
closed yet open to others
embracing life's loves

MY TRUNK! With veil, convent prayer books, crucifixes worn through the years and my bride of Christ wedding ring.

AFTERWORDS

~~6~~

Today you are you! That is truer than true!
There is no one alive who is you-er than you.

—Dr. Seuss

MANY HAVE ASKED ME THROUGH the years whether I'm sorry I entered the convent. My spontaneous and forever answer is "Oh no. I loved it." For me to enter was the right thing to do in 1958 and to leave was the right thing to do in 1971.

And to the question of whether I'm sorry I left the convent, which no one has ever asked, my answer would be similar. "Oh no. I needed to move on." Being in the convent today is not the same; its evolution has kept up with the times. Women who stayed through the changes and women who entered after me have transformed the culture. Although they remain vowed women pledging a life of poverty, chastity, and obedience, how they live each vow is defined for the twenty-first century. That is a story for them to tell, not me.

Thirteen years recalled fifty years ago. Those were my convent years— years that thrust me into an engaging world where I blossomed. Those years gave me transformative roots and wings.

Leaving *for* the convent was exhilarating and freeing. I didn't realize the stronghold Dad's style had on me until I was freed from it. As I look back on my decision to leave home, I realize it was one of the strongest rebellions I could have made against him. And yet, for the young woman I was, it was a safe and holy choice.

Leaving *from* the convent was different. Unlike in 1958, when I could hardly wait to press the Go button, walk up those Motherhouse stairs, and say yes to becoming a Sister, I felt a sadness and a loss mingled with a competing conflict. I wasn't looking for a Stop button. I knew it was time to go; I felt a sense of completeness having served God in religious life but held a restlessness to move beyond how I was living. I felt an overwhelming sense of uncertainty. The void I was stepping into was big and unknown: in split seconds I had signed papers that made me a lay woman, no longer accountable to vows.

The order and structure that my life held during my first thirty years was collapsing. I was left with questions and no one to give me answers. I felt on my own for the first time. It was scary and ultimately challenging and freeing.

It became clear soon after I left that my relationship with my dad changed. The battle of wills between us was over. Neither of us had anything to prove to the other. I liked being around him, and he loved to tell me stories of what he was doing and how things were going. Dad admired Harry, and our relationship was comfortable. He danced with me at my wedding. He was generous: he gave me a car—a forest-green Mercury Cougar. Later he built a garage for our LaGrange home where we raised our children. Unfortunately I lost him sooner than his death; he died of Alzheimer's at age seventy-eight. This strong, "in-charge" man forgot how to play checkers; he could be coaxed to go to his room by an offer of chewing gum.

Mom and I, on the other hand, grew into a relationship of unspoken competition. Once I became a mother, I assumed the very role that had consumed her life. She remained a bit distant from my children and would compare my lively bunch with her first grandchildren. "Tom's kids never acted so rowdy." And when I went back to school and worked outside the home, including traveling for the job, she questioned why I needed "all those degrees" and wondered why I couldn't just stay home and take care of the children. She would call and scold me for not calling her. She'd tell me all the things her sons were doing for her, especially my brother Bill. We never talked about this relational tension. Instead I reverted to the behaviors I had when I felt isolated from my dad's affection: I committed myself to my life—now, my own family and my work. As mom aged and needed more help, I defined my time with her as ministry, called to be a gentle, caregiving daughter: taking her out most Sundays—to church, to brunch, and then shopping.

I came to realize that Mom and Dad were the best parents they could be. Neither had known the affection of their fathers; their mothers were overburdened by family demands and had only so much energy to give. Even though I felt an emotional void where "I love you, Nancy," was not often spoken nor seldom demonstrated in physical embrace, I knew they gave me all that they could.

Harry entered my life when I had resolved that I could survive, live comfortably, and be content on my own. That my call to be a woman of service would continue and I would be fulfilled. I am forever blessed that we met, fell in love, and had the courage and commitment to marry.

My brothers three, each uniquely affectionate and loving, along with their wives, bring me great family joy. My own family, my husband, my son, Steve, and three daughters, Becky, Terri, and Lisa, with their life-committed partners, are genuinely caring for family and me. My four grandchildren, Clay, Foster, Charlie, and Benny, fill my senior years with delight and playfulness.

I cherished my convent years. I grew into womanhood, I grew as a woman of service, I grew so I am able to love freely and fully. My continued association with the Sisters of Saint Francis of Mary Immaculate keeps me rooted in what is important—living Franciscan values in and through the Gospel.

Today, only one school with which I served exists—Our Lady of Guadalupe. If not torn down like Saint Ludmilla, the other schools turned into parish centers or community-based missions. Another sign of change. Another era. Another call of ministry. May women of service today find their call and their way of being in the world so that we continue to love and serve others.

ACKNOWLEDGEMENTS

In loving gratitude for my husband, Harry, who has loved and encouraged me, a forever companion of generosity and love. To my four beautiful grandchildren, especially Foster, who now will know that his grandma as a nun was "someone," not "none-thing." To my four children and their life companions that they will continue to be the loving adults that they are, each of whom has found service an important part of who they are. May their spiritual sense of generosity and love grow. I wish to thank everyone who has encouraged me to write this memoir and especially thank those who helped me prepare it for publication. Special thanks to my beta readers, my husband and friends, Sister Ann Freiburg, Jeanne and Joe Foley. They did what I hoped for—they pulled apart my first draft and challenged its flow and message. The results, I trust, are truer now to what I wanted to say.

Special thanks to Sr. Marianne Saieg for her photography used on the cover and the picture of St. Pascal's walkway. And thank you to Shawn Sweeney for the timely nudge that got me writing.

Appendix A: Letters Home

Although we may be far apart, family is always close at heart.

—Anonymous

JMJF
January 25, 1959
Dear Mom and Dad,

I hope you had as nice day on your anniversary as you did for Dad's birthday. It's good that you're taking time off from building the new house to relax. How is the house coming along? I bet you're anxious to get it finished and move in.

How are you, Mom? I hope you're getting better. I'm sorry to hear that the boys, especially Tommy, aren't very helpful. Tommy should be able to do a lot for you.

It's only been a month since I last saw you and so much has happened since then. Our New Year's celebrations were loads of fun. New Year's Eve we had a miniature festival with small games going on in every corner. We decorated our room with crepe paper and the balloons you sent. The room sure looked festive.

We set the clock ahead so that at 8:30, it was midnight. Sister Zita was then crowned New Year's queen; with the singing of Auld Lang Syne we proceeded into the other room for refreshments. On New Year's Day we gave a play for the novices. I portrayed Sister Zita in one section, an Angel in another and Miss Nancy in another act. That's what you call a change of characters! In the evening, we had another party.

All the Christmas decorations came down on January 2 and our study looked again as a room or study. Before school started again, we saw the movie Caine Mutiny.

Today is a very big day for three girls and, in fact, all of us. Our postulant class will again number 26. We are getting Miss Martha, Ann and Joan. They will have the same ceremony we had. Tonight we're going to have a party for them to make them right at home.

Mom, Lucille Ruatto is being received into the BVMs as a novice on February 3; they only have six months of postulancy. She'd certainly appreciate a card. Her address is Mount Carmel Convent, Dubuque, Iowa.

There are three more visiting Sundays before my reception. The next one is February 8, then Easter Sunday and the last one is in June. You don't have to come for the full three hours, Mom, since the kids get so restless. Just let me know what time you plan to come. Visiting will be over at Tower Hall—the main entrance—so if I know the time I'll be waiting for you. If my income tax papers are ready, I'll sign them.

We've been talking pretty seriously about our Sister names. Sister Zita doesn't think I'll be able to get Victor Marie, but I don't know. I'm having a time choosing names, but what do you think of Sister Keith? Do you have any suggestions? It can be two names put into one or one name. I've got a lot of time yet.

Dear Tommy,

I'm waiting patiently to see if you're still living. Maybe a few questions will give you that extra push to write to your sis. How were your exams? They couldn't have been tougher than mine. Ours were scheduled for two hours a piece—but they are all over now.

I was talking to Father Aquinas today and he said you made a good grade in Religion. What about your other grades? I haven't received mine yet but if the results of the tests are any indication, I'm not too anxious.

Have you been going to the JCHS socials? Has Catholic High won very many basketball games? Did you hear the Academy is changing uniforms next year to brown and white? What school colors are those!!

That's all the questions for now—here's a little insight into what I've been doing.

Just before tests I played my first piano piece. You wouldn't believe it but I forgot where middle C was. What a mix-up! I guess I'm not musically inclined. My course in Music Theory is over and I'm going to start one in Art—lettering. It is very practical for teaching.

I'm also going to be taking Natural Science which has a lot of physics and chemistry and my first philosophy course in logic. Logic is a reasoning and thinking course. We'll have to explain why statements are false or why they are true. Take this for example: "All chests are boxes; a man has a chest so therefore it is a box." Sounds funny doesn't it? I finished my course in Algebra and Biology, but will still be taking the same course in Religion, English and History.

When you come up on Feb. 8, Tommy, would you bring up the rest of my notebooks except Algebra and Latin—you probably could use those. Please bring also my book reports; they're in a small brown folder. God love you.

Dear Billy,

Thank you so much for your cute letter. It looks like you got a real nice typewriter for Christmas. I'm glad you keep trying your best in school. I'm proud of you.

Billy, one of the new girls brought a hula hoop with her. I bet I get better than you. We're going to have a lot of fun with it.

Well, all, I guess I'd better close now. I'm looking forward to seeing all of you, Larry, Billy, Tommy, Dad and Mom.

With love,
Your Nancy

Easter 1959
Dear Everyone,

"Resurrexi" the liturgy sang this morning and its "Alleluia" note carries the day on a joyous tone. I've had a very joyous Easter. Your letters and cards were the "cream in the frosting." And, of course, the first candy of the Easter season tastes the best. Thanks, Mom and all.

Sister Stephen was in retreat here at the Motherhouse this past week and I visited with her today. She is what I'd call a "solid" Sister—I'm mighty proud to have her in our family.

Retreat brought a change in routine and what fun we had taking over first year duties. I was lucky enough to be one of the assistant cooks. Need any ideas for salads, Mom?

The retreat master introduced the "Better World" movement which you probably will be hearing about. Its aim is to promote unity among the Christians by showing love for each other. He suggested a resolution: "Not to lay your tongue on any person for a year." Quite a challenge! We were able to hear some of the conferences in between working and decorating.

Did you ever hear of the Russian bowl service, Mom? We tried it for our meal at dinner today. I helped organize it. We arranged our tables in banquet style and each Sister was presented her food by a server. The servers carried a bowl and placed it at the left of the Sister so she could help herself. One of the home economic teachers taught us how to serve formally. It was a wonderful experience and we all enjoyed it.

Tomorrow is going to be a busy day, so I hope to finish this letter tonight. In the morning we are having an egg hunt with the postulants and in the afternoon visiting with the professed Sisters. I still have to squeeze some study time in before Wednesday. School hops on us faster than the Easter rush of duties, but I console myself, there is a joy in learning.

Your daughter,
Nancy

April 12, 1959
Dear Mom and Dad,

Days—how fast they go by!!! In just two weeks, since I last talked to you much has happened.

On Easter Monday, the postulants had an egg hunt with the novices out on the campus. Can't you picture us hunting for our egg, looking up and down and around? We certainly had fun. I was one of the last to find mine—it was out in the middle of the yard—surprised it wasn't stepped on. We had the hunt in the morning and in the afternoon the postulancy was filled with Academy Sisters and other professed Sisters. It is always enjoyable to visit with the Sisters. Sister Margaret sends her hello.

Easter Tuesday brought with it many exciting Moments. The postulants, all 25 of us, Sister Zita and Sister Emeran, our Natural Science teacher, went to Chicago. We boarded the bus at 8:30 and came home at 4:30. We visited the Planetarium, Aquarium and the Natural History Museum. I think we were more on display than the exhibits. It isn't every day that postulants are seen in the world. What really topped the day was our picnic lunch on the Lake Shore front. It was nice enough to eat outside and so the postulants found ourselves picnicking right alongside Lake Michigan. Although all of us enjoyed the trip, everyone commented on how good it was to get back home. There is something about the convent, Dad, even though you can't understand, that makes living so desirable and peaceful.

Easter Wednesday, we found ourselves tackling the books once again. It was good to get back to our usual routine of studying.

That's enough on big days now to give you little tidbit of news.

First, Billy, I want to thank you for your package. I enjoyed it so much especially the picture of you. You sit on top my desk and I see it every time I study.

Thank Aunt Betty and Mary Ellen, Mom, for their package; personal supplies always come in handy.

Well, folks, two months from today, we find out if we'll be accepted by Reverend Mother into the novitiate. That will be a big day. Soon we will have to have our names ready. Everyone is getting serious about picking three choices. I've been going through my daily missal, saints' books and baby books trying to find some names. All forms, at least all the pretty forms of Thomas, William are taken.

Your loving Nancy

May 10, 1959
Hi, Everyone!

Writing Sunday caught me at a very busy time—I have a short story due tomorrow and I've got a long way to go on it. There's so very much to tell you; I better get started.

First, Mom, I hope you had a very happy day. We celebrated Mother's Day grandly here. I hope you liked the prayer card I made for your prayer book. Right now at 12:30, you're probably at Aunt Betty's house. Tell Mary Ellen I've been thinking about her today and picturing her in her pretty white dress. I hope the party turned out successful.

Before I go on with my tidbits of news, Dad, I have to tell you—your letter made me so very happy.

How has the law case progressed? Don't worry about it, Dad, things will work out for the best—just wait and see. And Dad—don't give up eating—I want to see you on visiting Sunday. Your new car is just beautiful; I love the colors—it looks like you're riding in luxury. I guess I have to wait until Sunday to give you a great big hug, but you deserve it now for everything.

Sister Zita and I think if you bring Mary Ellen and Billy at 3:00 on May 17, it will work out fine. It can be only a very short visit—because it is a special one—about 10 minutes, but I do want to see the little ones dressed in their white.

Billy, make a real good First Communion. I'll be praying for you.

After our special visit, June 7 is the next visiting Sunday—then there are no more until August 13. The time is the same 1:00 to 4:00. Relatives and friends are invited.

Love,
Nancy

JMJF
June 16, 1959
My dear Daddy,

Just a little note to tell you I love you and to wish you a very "Happy Father's Day." The wallet I made could never contain all the feelings I want to express, but I hope you enjoy it.

Last week was a week of leisure for us. Just a few odd jobs and the rest of the time was spent outside playing games or mending. Although only Tuesday this week proved to be quite different. The postulants have the honor of serving the meals for the Sisters on retreat. If I begin to relate stories of what has happened so far I wouldn't have enough paper. I bet, though, a lot of things that have happened to us would be quite familiar to Mom in her "service days."

Just a couple of minutes ago, I was measured for the holy habit. It is hard to believe that I'll be a Sister in less than two months.

Daddy, I know you'll be a "proud papa" on August 13 for I'm mighty proud of him myself. No matter how many times I thank you, I never feel satisfied, in just saying "Thanks" for letting me come.

Again, Daddy, "Happy Father's Day." I hope you "live it up."

With all my love,

Your favorite daughter,

Nancy

JMJF

July 7, 1959

Dear Mom and Dad,

Emerging from Metaphysics and the principle, "Is I is or Is I not," I sit down and write to my favorite family. Besides the challenging philosophy course of Metaphysics, I am taking a delightful speech course—the title of our book is "Speech Without Tears." Well, in one short paragraph, you can see how I've been spending my time the past two weeks and how I will be kept busy until the end of July. We attend class in the morning with a 45 minute break between courses. The afternoon is spent mainly in study and the evening in both study and free time.

Before I go on about myself I want to be sure you had a swell Father's Day, Dad and you, Mom, a happy birthday. I'm sure you did. Did you like the cards? My embroidery work is still the results of a beginner, but at least the colors are pretty, yes?

I was certainly surprised to say the least to see you at the cornerstone laying. You all looked so good. Did you like our singing?

In my letter to Dad I mentioned the serving we did. Was it ever a delightful week! I was in charge of the dining room with all the little old Sisters—they were so precious to wait on. We all wore heavily starched white aprons, pushed carts around and looked mighty efficient. At the close of retreat, the Jubilee celebrations took place. Tommy will remember them very well. It was certainly inspiring to see Sisters who lived as Sisters 50 and 60 years receive their crown of flowers. Some of them showed signs of living many more years in the service of the Lord.

I met or at least saw most of Tommy's grade school teachers. I worked with Sister David Ann; I've seen Sister Jovita and Billy would be interested—I saw Sister Concepta during retreat and Sister Paul Ann goes to the college this summer. Tommy, do you remember Sister Theodette—she remembers you quite well—she said she'll never forget you and the yo-yo on her feast day. By the way, you should see her play volleyball.

July 4th we had a volleyball game—temporary professed Sisters vs. postulants and novices. We won! I was hoping that you'd ride by that day—the campus was full of Indians, Pandas (dressed up postulants and Sisters), floats, hand rockets, stars, decorations and what have you—a parade! The parade circled the campus and stopped at the volleyball court. There the game was held. Cheers and music resounded throughout the groups. To top the day we had an outside barbeque with the novices. It is certainly one fourth of July, I'll never forget.

Saturday will be another exciting day—Community Day at the Academy. There will be skating, visiting and a dinner highlighting activities. It is also the day the Sisters change their veils—so if you see a strange set of nuns walking around town it will probably be our Sisters.

Well, I think I've hit on all the news but I've saved the biggest and best item of interest until last.

RECEPTION DAY is just a little over a month away. I've been fitted for my wedding dress and my habit. All our preparations are for the big day. I'll be writing again before retreat, but just so you know what everything is about I tell you now, too.

You, Mom and Dad, will receive two white tickets that will admit you to the Cathedral and the dinner at Tower Hall. The boys and a few quests *(will be up to you) will receive colored tickets which will admit them to the Cathedral and the dinner.*

Parents have reserved seats in front. Pictures will be taken about 9:00 of the group of us in our gowns and the procession to the Cathedral will begin at 9:10 on August 13ᵗʰ. You will be able to watch the procession and take pictures of it (and me). The ceremonies are long, Dad, so be prepared! They will probably last until 11:30-12:00. Right after, you go to Tower Hall for dinner and then visiting is from 1:00-4:30. Encourage all my relatives (your side, too, Dad) to at least stop and see me. Visiting will be on the campus, but this time come and get me first at the front door. We can walk out there together. A supper is served to you and the guests outside and visiting begins again at about 6:30 and ends at 8:00. Please arrange so that, just the family have a little time for ourselves in the evening. OK, folks?

If you are wondering what to get JoAnn, a book would probably be a good idea. Mrs. Kietzman at Joyce's Religious Shop could give you some ideas. Maybe something on the Holy Spirit, St. Joseph or St. Maria Goretti would be good.

Mom, when you get a chance—reception would be soon enough— will you buy me a roll or two of scotch tape (.59 size to fit in dispenser) and some cement glue? Thanks. As far as other supplies—it would be a good idea to have enough of everything in advance for my cloister year.

Back to study for me! Keep smiling, keep happy and I'll be seeing you soon—as a novice. Love, Nancy

521 Plainfield Rd.
Joliet, IL
October 4, 1959
Dear Mom, Dad, Tommy, Billy and Larry,
    It's Christmas in October! Well, almost—it is St. Francis Day in the convent and although it's dreary outside, a merry spirit prevails inside— and presents besides—what a happy surprise. Thanks to you wonderful

people! I thought I'd send you a part of our refectory decorations. This "birdie" was on my nut cup.

Peace and everything good to you—a true Franciscan hello to all of you. I've been thinking about you so very much since reception day and, I must admit, missing you, too.

How is the law case coming, Dad? I was hoping I'd hear some good news. Don't forget your promise!! Your "little novice daughter" hasn't seen her Dad's handwriting for a long time! Ahem—hint.

And Mom—you're probably as busy as ever just planning meals and keeping all our men-folk in order. When you have time please write me a long letter to let me know how you feel and how everyone else is. Aunt Betty told me about herself in a real nice letter.

Oh, before I forget, Mrs. Ujcik sent a picture of me in my wedding dress. It is a beautiful picture, a little shaded by the trees, but the unique thing about it is that you, Mom, Dad and Larry are in the background and Daddy is taking my picture. It is in color and you can be seen in that pretty blue dress very well.

Speaking of reception, just one more big THANK YOU to everyone who made my day so memorable by visiting and bringing packages. I especially like my trunk cover, Mom; you must have put a lot of work into it. The material is beautiful and it fits well.

Tommy, I miss those old-after-school talks we used to have, but you really supplement them with delightful letters. You certainly have a rough schedule this year, but your social life will make up for the drudgery of homework. Now that you're taking German and I've heard so much about it from the Second Year Novices, I'm going to suggest it for my language next year. Have to hold onto the German in us, you know. How's this for a starter:

"Gentes haltet Euch gut beim Tanz!"

So you have Sister Raymarie this year, Billy? I know you like her. She is a very nice Sister (and quite capable of handling Billy, Mom). I hope you study well this year, Billy and be good. I'm expecting a letter from you soon; Sister Raymarie told me you're writing.

And little Larry, I can't forget you, although you're really not that "little" anymore. Be a good boy and help Mom all you can. Do you still have the scar where you fell?

Switching over to "520's side of town," I'd like to give you some of the "behind the scene" happenings of Sister Victor Marie. She certainly is a girl of a variety of chores and the like.

At barbeques, you'd find me caught in a whirl of smoke as I flip over the hamburgers and drop the onion and cheese on our favorite dinner.

Already you can tell my favorite job is around food. I love to work in the kitchen and I never tire of peeling or even washing pots. Once in a while we help the cooks bake, but most of the time we prepare the meat, potatoes and vegetables. As novices we have the added honor of serving the professed and ourselves. You know how bustling a kitchen can be at meal time, Mom, well, you can imagine the situations we find ourselves in sometimes—oops milk spilled, wipe it up, oh here comes the dessert—the hot food is starting to be served...But I love every minute of it.

Besides kitchen, you'll find me in the laundry. I and another Sister are in charge of sorting and getting the machines started for the big week's wash. And Saturday, Sister Maria Goretti and I have the privilege of ironing altar linens.

Your novice daughter does more than work, although she loves it all. She prays and especially does she pray for her family. Every day I say my five decade rosary for you—one decade for each member of my family. Of course, our cloistered year is centered around prayer and religious ideals. Our main study this year is the vows and constitution of our community.

School is only a four-day week this year and we attend school right in the novitiate study room. We have courses in religious poetry, Christian virtues, the liturgy and Gregorian chant. Sister Anacleta, our mistress, instructs us in the vows and constitutions and has informal classes in Bible History and Manners. It is an easy year so that our time may be centered on prayer.

And do I recreate—with 48 Sisters living together we never tire for things to do. The novitiate is mighty proud of our band which has 13 members. It is really good—although I can't play I give encouragement. Before school started, we had what is called the annual "Play Day." The campus was transformed into a picnic grounds. All day we were free to do anything we wanted—tennis, volley ball, etc. The day ended with a barbeque. Cards and mending take up recreation time mostly.

A few novitiate customs you'd probably be interested in are that we receive mail the first, third and if there is one, the fifth Sundays of the month; packages we usually receive as they come in, but we write notes on Sunday. In Advent we won't be receiving mail or packages, but I'll be expecting a real long letter from all of you at Christmas. It seems a long way off, but I'll be writing then again.

It is now October 5! Good Morning! I was hoping if I "slept on my letter" I wouldn't forget anything. You haven't asked me any questions, so I don't know if I've told you all the interesting news.

Today is still a day of celebration—we visit with the postulants and professed. This will be the first time I'll be seeing Sister Margaret since reception. (by the way, her feast day is October 17.)

My paper is coming to an end but one more thing. To tell you that my life is a bed of roses with no thorns would be quite unbelievable. I didn't give up being human when I entered the convent and little headaches and heartaches come, but they are in any life. I am very happy to be here.

Keep happy and healthy and remember your girl with the pretty name of Sister Victor Marie.

JMJF
521 Plainfield Rd.
Joliet, IL
November 15, 1959
Dear Mom and Dad,

Surprised to hear from me? So am I! That is one of the joys of convent living—you never know when the unexpected will come.

I was so glad to hear from you today and that cute letter from Larry was sweet. Did he write it himself?

There are so many things I want to say: I'm mighty proud of Aunt Betty and very anxious to see her. I'm sorry to hear about Uncle Marty— I'm praying for him…and I hope nothing is seriously wrong with Uncle Al. I'm very glad to hear that you're going to the Mother's Club, Mom; that is a tremendous outlet to everyday routine.

Billy, thank you for your letter. I heard you're getting along well in school. Keep it up and be good to Sister Raymarie.

Aunt Irma wrote me a real nice letter and sent a typical picture of little Timmy. It is so nice to hear from her. Aunt Betty also wrote and is as sweet as ever.

Dearest Daddy, I'm looking over the last letter you wrote and I don't think I'll ever be able to understand you completely. Be assured that I'm not losing any weight and I have run out of ways to let you know that I am content and happy and mighty anxious to share my joys in the classroom. I may express myself poorly but I hope you will someday understand.

Tommy, your last letter was precious; I enjoyed reading it immensely. It sounded like you had a good time at the dance. You're turning out to be a well-rounded kid—stay that way and I'll always be proud of you.

Now a little bit about your cloistered Nancy. I really don't feel too cloistered, in fact, I've been over to the Cathedral twice since I wrote last. We attended two important Masses that were held there.

In the play we gave for Mother Borromeo this year I played the part of Lady Poverty in a very solemn scene and in one of the following scenes I was a fierce barbarian who falls to the ground dead. It was a play on Saint Clare and in the last scene I was a virgin in heaven. Quite a variety of parts, wouldn't you say? Plays and programs are always a joy to prepare.

Oh, Dad, I must tell you, on the memorable day of October 27, I ate my first turnips. Now I am truly initiated into the convent. By the way, I didn't have sauerkraut with it.

Do you know I'm not waiting to enter a classroom to begin teaching? I've started right in the novitiate. One of my classmates has a rough time with her English grammar and spelling, so once a week we meet for class. I love to do it and I'm improving my own as I go along. Don't judge my grammar in this letter, though. I'm writing rather hastily.

Thanksgiving is coming fast and it looks like winter is here to stay. Be sure to thank the good God for putting me here. I thank Him for you every day.

I can picture so well the little ones scanning the Christmas catalogs. That was always a joy. Although I don't need much, I've thought of a few things since last time. My stamp supply is running low and I broke my manicure scissors, so pretty please. Don't send me anything I can't use because I really haven't the place to put it and you waste your money. Take it easy, stay happy and healthy.

With love for all of you,
Sister Victor Marie

JMJF
December 26, 1959
Dear Family,

Being remembered fills me with much joy—Mom and Dad's sincere and lovable letters, Tommy's humorous one and the little ones wishes all were wonderful. My gifts, too, show that they were sent with devoted love. I'm going to use the money for my dentist bills, Dad. I've had one appointment and three more to come in January with Dr. Wilhelmi, whose office is right down the street. I think the bill will be at least $20.00. Ugh! Expensive daughter you have! The cookies are delicious, Mom. I especially like the round chocolate nut. At Christmas we're able to keep 2 lbs. of sweets for ourselves. My Mom's cookies are part of the 2 lbs. to be sure!

FLASH! My mistress just called me into the office. There two beautiful cakes sit and 12 cans of punch. Oh, you people, what can I tell you, but thanks, thanks so much. I want to hug all of you. Tonight after prayer, we're going to have the treat—thank you so very much.

Back to my Christmas and more thanks—the book is beautiful and a life-long keepsake. It looks like you want to keep me nice and cozy with those socks. They will! And, of course, the supplies will always be put to good use.

Adding to all your wonderful wishes, I got many cards from our relatives and friends: Aunt Betty sent delicious cookies and supplies; Aunt Irma, candy, Aunt Mary, note paper and a small manicure set, Uncle Joe and Aunt Mary, money, the Witczaks, nylons and the Designors, a box of sweets.

Although I'll be sending notes, make sure you tell them all that I appreciate their thoughtfulness and good wishes.

I have one special wish that you, my family, could be here in the convent for Christmas. I would like to share with you all the peace and happiness that fills these halls. I think a little bit of heaven is experienced during this holy season. I know you'll never forget how inspiring the midnight Mass you attended here was. After hours of choir rehearsals, the beauty of the human voice reaches its heights at Mass. After Mass, we first years, were led into a beautifully decorated room, a room we weren't permitted to enter for two days. Sister Anacleta and the second years had trimmed a 12ft tree and a crib, supplied us with Santa stockings and dressed our desks with presents and wishes from home. I went to bed at 2:30 and found myself in chapel again at 6:00. We attended two more Masses, at both of which I remembered all of you especially. The rest of the day was spent in visiting the Sisters and postulants, looking at leach others' gifts and just making merry. What's in store for the following days is a surprise for us but the holiday season will prevail until school comes again.

I started this letter at 10:00 on my birthday. It is now 1:00, December 27. Time flies. Since I started I got another present: Aunt Theresa sent a nice box of cookies, beautiful cards and some Avon.

I had just a wonderful birthday. They get better every year, I think. Some of the Sisters told me they wish I'd have a birthday next week, too. Aunt Betty's cake was delicious and I sampled the other one, too. I don't know how to thank you enough.

There is so much to tell all of you I'm going to write your notes separately on the next page.

Dear Mom,

I just finished rereading your letter. It is so filled with interesting notes which all spell Christmas joy. I'm so very glad. The gifts the family gave you must have made you happy. They sounded beautiful. You can add my love.

Since I wrote last I have been developing many womanly arts. The main one is the art of peeling. Remember how clumsy I was at home? My left hand didn't seem to function as well as your right. Now I can eye a potato as fast as a "cat can wink his eye." I've been learning many different ways of making salads and the like. This Christmas I practiced my art of baking by helping make chocolate chip and cinnamon cluster cookies. I still like your chocolate chip better.

You didn't mention how you feel so I'm hoping that means better. My prayers are with you and the family always.

Dear Dad,

That good news you wrote about has really touched the curious side of me. I hope "soon" comes fast.

Being a carpenter's daughter certainly comes in handy. Before Christmas I helped put up our outside crib, not the front crib, but on the novice grounds. It was good to have a hammer and nails in hand. Around the crib we put Christmas trees which were a challenge to figure out how to keep them standing.

I brought the pictures of our new house in from the trunk for Christmas. I want to show them to my mistress. Her Dad was a contractor, too.

I really appreciate your warm Christmas wishes, Dad. You're tops.

I'm still praying for the Johnson business and wishing it will come out for the best and soon.

Sister Stephen's mother is sick yet and is now at St. Joseph's hospital. I'm going to write to Sister Stephen when I finish this letter.

Dear Tommy,

I've been hearing many a tale about my "little brother." It sounds like you've made quite a name for yourself among SFA's sophomores. That picture of you is quite a "knockout" itself.

Your letter and your cards had me in stitches. I enjoyed your narration of the saleswomen. Very typical.

Do you consider yourself a "pro" yet in the accordion field? I hope I can hear you in August.

Well, enjoy yourself these holidays. It looks like you will have a merry time.

In case I have no more opportunities to write before your birthday, I want to wish you a very happy one. Maybe your dream car will become a reality.

Dear Billy and Larry,

Sister Raymarie tells me you're doing fine, Billy. She said you find some things harder but that's all right. Just do your best.

I thought of you both very much this Christmas and I hope Santa was very good to you.

Did you really write your letter, Larry, or did Billy help you? It looks so nice. You're doing well in your writing, Billy.

Both of you—be really good and make your Sister proud of you (or should I say prouder?)

My paper is coming to the bottom, but my Christmas cheers are still high for all of you. I pray that this will be your happiest, holiest holiday season.

I'm including a few things that I could use, Mom, but please don't send them right away—none are desperately needed.

Again—merry, merry, merry Christmas holidays and may the New Year bring much peace and joy into the Polyak dwellings.

With all my love,
Sister Victor Marie
Nancy

520 Plainfield Rd.
Joliet, IL
Easter 1960
My dear family,

I can't think of a very fancy way of saying it, but I hope when this letter reaches you, you will have had a very happy Easter. Today was everything good it could be except a visit from you. I only wish you could share the peace that was mine this Holy Week and, of course, it was climaxed today.

I got Easter greetings from Judy Horvatin, Aunt Betty, Aunt Anne and the Witczaks—all wishing me the best. In my last letter I promised I'd remember all my relatives in prayer, especially during Lent and I did just that. I remembered every family on a special day and you'd be surprised how much I thought of them. I was wondering how Uncle Joe is; how Tony and Katherine are living; what Mary Jane's baby's name is (I forgot—but congrats for the coming little one—congratulations also Jeannette and Uncle Mike); is Uncle Arnie still building? You answered my questions about Joey—in Germany!! I thought of Marty and hoped he is getting better.

As I write this a group of Sisters are around the piano singing "In your Easter bonnet." I've been reading some "holy thoughts" about the origin of our Easter customs and their singing reminded me to pass them on to you. All of Easter suggests "putting on the new man" or more commonly known—beginning to live a more God-centered life. That's what the new Easter bonnets and clothes are to symbolize. The Easter parade was originally an Easter procession after Mass. Mr. Bunny coming from his ground home symbolizes Christ rising from His tomb! Easter eggs are to remind us again of this "new life." Interesting, yes?

Sister Raphael is standing in the doorway and has just told me to send my Mom Easter greetings. She said to tell you I'm "almost as good as Alma Kump was. Sister has been wonderful in directing our Easter music for the novitiate choir—it was beautiful.

By now you can tell the novitiate is in a hustle of activity. Sister Anacleta is busy answering doorbells and receiving guests and packages.

Some of us are attempting to be the first to write our letters. Most of the Sisters are reading letters and opening packages or just enjoying each other's company. It is almost time for afternoon Vespers so my letter will again be interrupted.

Mom, I can't believe our "little one" is to start school. His sweet notes certainly sound like he is growing up. Sister Regine (Juanita) saw you and Larry downtown when she went to the dentist. Larry was bundled in his blue coat and Sister said he was getting big. His Easter outfit should make him a smart looking gentle man.

Bill, keep working hard at your arithmetic. I'm sure you'll do all right. Keep your Daddy busy helping you! (Sister Raymarie told me that Dad helped more than she did—and she also added that Billy looks mighty sharp in his red pants. Are you the president of the 3W Club, Bill? I hope this "willing worker" remembers his Mom.

April 22 is coming fast, Billy. Eat a big piece of cake for me. My, you're growing up, too—9 years old. Have fun at your party and I'll be thinking of you.

I didn't know I had a celebrity for a brother? By the time you read this you will have already performed, Tommy, but I wish you the best of everything. Tom, I enjoyed your letter so much—activities—sports and dances—spells sophomore and I think you're living it well. (Lots of fun, isn't it?) Now that this "old woman" looks back on her high school days, I think Soph memories are the most cherished.

A very special thanks for the supplies and sweets, Mom (chocolates hit the spot after Lent.) I'm afraid I don't have room for the file box. It's my fault for not describing it better. One of the Sisters has a 4x6x4 size in wood and it is perfect for book reports. Do you think you could pick up the one you sent at the 520 door and perhaps return it? I'm sorry.

Dad, Sister Anacleta told me about your accident during Lent...and the law suit trouble. Daddy, is it really worth all the trouble you're going through? It's a month now since you wrote so I hope things are better. I was sorry to hear about the accident, but glad to hear you didn't get hurt.

Dad, could I ask you something special? Will you make your Easter duty this year? Nothing would please me more.

A few of the novices saw you drive through yesterday. I couldn't have been farther away. I was at the other end of the building decorating our refectory. Sister Maria Goretti's folk drove through today just as we were all walking through the laundry room. They got a wave from the whole novitiate (and a few extra from JoAnn.)

I was very delighted to see you the other day, though. That was my Easter treat. Well, four months isn't very long when you look at what's past. Is it? But…I am look forward to seeing you face-to-face.

Well, how about some news from this side? With little explanation, I think you know what novices in a big house like this were doing before Easter. One thing especially worth writing about is the day I was the cook or I should say the day four of us took the cook's place? Thank the Lord the baker was still home. Two of the Sisters fried meat and Sister Lora and I made the salad. (Even a Jell-O salad is a major project in a house of 140 Sisters.) When the dinner was under control we proceeded to help with the baking. While the other Sisters made ginger snaps, Sister Lora, my laundry partner and I tried a new recipe called princess squares. It actually turned out terrific. No major mishaps occurred and I had a very enjoyable day. I enjoy working in the kitchen more each day. There is much to learn. One day while I was cleaning chickens (just the final steps, believe me). I couldn't help remembering the time Daddy killed one of our chickens on Pasadena Ave. I can still see the fellow running around headless and feathers flying. Ugh!

Easter Tuesday

I could kick myself for not finishing this; you'd have my letter by now. I don't want to waste space explaining but yesterday was our visiting day with the Sisters and in the evening we saw a movie—"Never Take No for an Answer." It was darling.

Today we visit with postulants and have our annual egg hunt. We have free tomorrow yet and then back to the old grind. I have still a lot of mending to catch up with.

We said good-bye to an old reliable friend that I must tell you about. By "we" I mean five of the novices who have the Dish Pantry as a morning charge. The old friend was a worn out Dish Pantry machine. All of a sudden he couldn't take anymore and plans were made for getting a new one. During the two months before Easter, novices were seen washing dishes by hand while watching the development of the new Dish Pantry—walls were torn down, cupboards restored, a new floor installed and old Victor (brand name) met his burial ground. Now we're back in our new kitchen after weeks of coughing sawdust, etc. The machine is beautiful, but so far we're still adjusting to it.

Here I am again almost at the end of my letter. There is so much to tell you about. It will be a long time before I write again. In fact I don't think I'll be writing anymore letters unless something unexpected comes before visiting day. Don't forget, I want so much to have a little time with "just the family." You're the ones I miss the most. Be sure to take care of yourself. Mail comes to us every first, third and fifth Sundays so I'll be looking forward to hearing from you.

A very happy birthday to Billy. Love to all. I'm glad "love" has no weight—I'd have a mighty heavy package to send home this time if it did. Stay good, Tom.

Lovingly,
Nancy

JMJF
October 6, 1960
Dear Family,

Peace and everything good from your Franciscan daughter and sister. I know everything good is yours. Mom's back home. I'm so glad for you, Mom, but now take it easy. You probably have felt some of that Franciscan spirit around the house lately. After all, Franciscanism is a spirit of charity and love. (You can tell Aunt Betty that she's a pretty good Franciscan.)

It must be different to have all the boys in school. Mom. How's Larry doing in his pronunciation? Billy in Reading? And Tommy in everything? Tom, how about telling me yourself?

By the way, I can't let this letter get any farther without telling you—I heard about you. I won't build up your ego, but I will tell who mentioned you to me. First, 21 of my wonderful classmates, second Sister Cyrinus, my mistress and third one of the college girls. You get around. Really, though, in all seriousness I am sorry I missed you at the stadium and very glad to hear about you. (My cold is all gone now.)

August seems so very long ago, doesn't it? That was a wonderful visiting day. Many thanks to all who came and for all the sweet-tooth fillers. You know, I could get spoiled with all the attention you gave me. But again thanks to everyone. How is Jackie doing at St. Francis? I saw the new handbook and it looks swell.

September's passed and October and the school year are in full swing. It was really delightful to go back to school and having a full schedule I'm kept very busy, to say the least. My schedule consists of Journalism (I already have some stories), Poetry (by now you can see, I'm to be an English major—three cheers), German I (a lot of work, but fun, too), General Psychology (I'm learning what is life from the philosophical side—fascinating), History of American Education and Scripture.

Now for some stories. My first Journalism assignment brought me to the desk of the president of the college. I had a twenty minute interview with her and I found it very relaxing and interesting. My second assignment was to find and interview four college girls whose mothers went to CSF. I had only their names, but beginners luck was with me. I found no trouble interviewing them. Right now I'm reviewing books—one is a rare copy of Hopkins's poems.

Being a member of the Interlude, *the College paper makes me feel obliged to ask you to buy a subscription. It is $1.50, but you certainly aren't obliged to accept. You will, though, see "Sister Victor Marie" in print once in a while, I hope. Like I said, the school year is on and the pink slip is another proof.*

Have you been hearing bells this week, convent bells, that is? Yours truly is ringing them this week. That's another story. It was my turn last week to ring the rising bell, well, you know how I like to sleep…

It was 5:00 Thursday morning—5:05-5:07 no bell had rung. At 5:10 in the morning I heard the bell, but I wasn't pulling the rope. Who was? I didn't know but I jumped out of bed and made a record-breaking dressing in 10 minutes. When I arrived down to chapel only the silence of the halls was mine. I went to chapel with quite a disturbed mind. It was only later in the day that I found out who rang it—a professed Sister who was awakened by our nurse. I resolved always to wind my clock from henceforth.

As a second year novice tradition, we put on a play for the enjoyment of the old and young Sisters on October 4ᵗʰ. The college is getting ready for Showboat, you know, so on part of a boat we had "Francis Goes to the East." I only wish you could see one of our productions. They are rare. We had Arabian slaves, crusaders, friars and Saracens with costumes to match.

October 7, 1960

School, prayer, etc. etc., stop the progress of this letter, but I resolve to finish tonight.

I just saw my first TV program since I entered 520—the Nixon-Kennedy Debate. Are they ever good! I only wish I could vote in this election. I think it is going to be a rough choice. If you wonder what my reactions to seeing TV was—I haven't many. It's odd, but that's one thing I never missed seeing. Speaking of TV, do you know they are planning a nation-wide education program for TV? If it goes into effect there will be many changes in the average classroom.

There is a little change in visiting days. I better write it now less I forget. We have two more visiting Sundays before August 12. It is up to you when you want to come, but I'd like to scatter the two times more or less proportionately. The times are as follows;

1. *Any Sunday before Advent except 1ˢᵗ Sunday of the month—not November 6.*
2. *Or any Sunday after Christmas until Lent except Jan. 8 and Feb. 5*
3. *And any Sunday after Easter except May 7 until June.*

The first Sunday of the month is a retreat day for us. Let me know, at least some idea, when you will be coming next. The time is the same 1:00 to 4:00 and please, Mom, no friends.

Dad, Mom, it's been said before that the longer you are in religion, the happier you are. I certainly can add a nod of the head and a reassuring yes to that.

School is somewhat of a pressure this year and it probably will continue to be, but I'm happy in spite of it and maybe even because of it. Every day I learn more about living properly—peacefully.

Well, I better be getting back to that "school work" but first a few more tidbits.

Sister Margaret's Dad died after a very long illness. By the way, Tom, do you see Sister in school?

Mom, if you come across gift wrapping ideas in Woman's Day or any other magazine, will you send them up? In fact even gift-making ideas would be of interest to the novices. The extent of my artistic talent lies in wrapping them only.

Do you know I haven't seen my reception pictures yet?

Tom, if you don't write soon I'll be asking, "Wie heissen, Sie?" How's life? School and otherwise? Be good to Mütterchen. Maybe by next letter I'll be able to write all in German. (I can dream.)

And, Billy, how do you like your teacher and school? Are you doing well?

I hope everything is all right with Aunt Mary in Chicago and with everyone. All—take care, especially you, Mom. A big thanks to Aunt Betty from me.

With love and prayers for all,
Sister Victor Marie

November 22, 1960
My dear family,

It is near holiday time again and the days won't let one catch up with them. I'm looking forward to Thanksgiving and its free days to try to "catch up" on some relaxation as well as heavy studying.

I'll be thinking about you Thursday and telling the Lord many thanks for having you as my family. Have a happy day. Don't eat too much!

Looking over your October letter, I see the end of that month closed with a household of sickness. I hope the end of this month will prove to be more pleasant. Your last letter was filled with many delightful things, Mom. I could see all of you so clearly at 1413.

Congratulations to Bob and Mary Jane. I hope Barb has recovered from her eye operation. Jackie Adams wrote me a delightful letter relating the problems of SFA living—very typical. Please tell her a very special thanks for buying the Focus for me. It was very thoughtful of her. I hope all my relatives are well.

How is Billy doing in school? And in general? I read an interesting article on how to understand eight to ten year olds. They live by conforming to the gang rules and want to be considered an important part of the family. Remind me to tell you more about it on visiting day.

And—speaking of visiting—when are you coming to see me? You didn't mention anything in your last letters, Mom, so I don't know what your plans are. Please let me know in your Christmas letter. (Don't forget Jan. 8 and first Sundays of the month are retreat Sundays.)

Having visiting inside more or less limits the space and so it would probably be wiser to eliminate inviting all my relatives. Maybe on August 12, we could all get together again.

If you are wondering what to get me—please don't, Mom. I really don't need anything. I know it's an act of charity on your part to buy Avon products from Aunt Mary, but I'm really not supposed to use highly scented powders. In our instructions we're learning more and more about the vow of poverty and I want to live it the best I can. Remind me to explain when we visit.

Just a little note now. With this vow, we never have to worry about our needs being taken care of—they are. But when it comes to extras—we share them. If you want to get me Christmas gifts, I would appreciate it if I could share them. Right now you're probably scratching your head and saying what is she talking about, how about it, Dad? I don't want to force any ideas on you, but for future reference—nuns do appreciate "community gifts." They could include books (I won't give any titles because I know it's a headache to chase after them) or records. In other words "something for the house—but goodness, nothing elaborate.

Do you know—journalism must be going into my bloodstream. I just reread what I wrote to you and I've given you "nothing but the facts." Bear with me, please. My "cold style" has to melt somewhat.

Let me tell you about my trip to the printer's shop. Two girls, Sister Seraphim (my journalism teacher) and I went to the Joliet Republic Printing Shop on the other side of town. It was fascinating. While Sister settled some business, we were busy watching the workmen. I felt so small next to all the printing machines. The manager showed me how to work the type machine by typing my name. I now have a permanent plate.

I love to write and there is such a satisfaction in seeing my "creation" in print. I had an article in the Herald News last month. Writing is really a sharing in God's creation—making something out of nothing.

Tom, speaking of writing—ich habe keinen Brief von Ihnen, nicht wahr? What are you going to do with your accordion now? What's "her" name? How's Deutsch? (I love it!) How's school? Wie ist meine Familie? I won't expect a written book by Christmas, but a chapter would be nice— how about it, Bruder?

Some very special Christmas gifts I want are first a very happy family to visit me (that I'm assured of); a nursery rhyme Larry can recite, a detailed account of how the family is, especially my Mother, what my Daddy is doing (I dreamt I was buying you a Christmas gift the other night), how Junior year is treating Tom and, last but not least, a loving brother by the name of Billy. I'll be good till Christmas, honest!

All 43 novices and Sister Cyrinus are well—no one has the flu this year. United with all their prayers for you, I am

Your loving daughter,

Sister Victor Marie

PS. We receive mail until Sunday. (NOTE: added to my letter probably by my novice mistress, Sister Cyrinus, reminding me that our letter were read before sending.)

The letter above is the last letter Mom saved. I didn't make copies of the letters I wrote to them. Throughout my convent years, I saved close to nothing—a practice I embraced even before I entered the community and far into my years as a religious woman. That everything had to fit in my trunk each time I was to move was an enticement to not save. And beyond sensitivity to physical space, I worked to model Saint Francis, who stripped himself of all earthly things to serve God. It is a discipline that nags at me yet today. I am ready to abandon most things, sometimes before it is practical to do so. I am grateful that I placed several treasures in my trunk that have helped yield this memoir, an aching story I felt urged to tell.

Appendix B: More Interlude Articles

Cruel world ignores
problems of left-handed

It's just no use trying—this is a right-handed world and nothing a left-handed person can do will persuade others that they are all wrong.

John and James' mother in the New Testament knew the left-hand position held its place and, at that, for all eternity. But it's taken nearly twenty centuries for tne world to see it since then.

It's a sad state of affairs when 11% of America's population (not to mention other countries) find they live in a wrong-sided world, with the odds being on the wrong side.

Occupations are limited—soda jerks use right-handed ice cream scoops; seamstresses have right-handed scissors . . . Then there are, of course, the fine arts—Ah! what educated person, left-handed or not, doesn't like the fine arts? But there's a 'techcinal' difficulty even in the creation of the beautiful: right-handed pen points for the artist, right-handed violins for the musician. It's a one-sided world, all right!

With all this, no wonder psychologists study the problem of frustrated left-handed people. The world rubs elbows with its left-handed neighbor and cares little about the friction. Maybe someday, just maybe there will be a panacea but until then it will mean living in a clumsy world.

—Sister Victor Marie, O.S.F.

The Interlude, October 12, 1961. Image courtesy of the Laverne and Dorothy Brown Library Archives, University of St. Francis, Joliet, IL.

We were born to love; sacrifice

Born in a period of hatred, we, the war babies, paradoxically enough were born to love.

Love began our life. An act of God shared through the love of parents made you and me.

Love sustained our life. Mom bent over the cradle, Dad paced the floor (or was it the other way around?) while you and I grew in security and love.

Security taught us to love—first Mom, then Dad, then the rest of the family (in between the hair tugging and pillow throwing times).

It was through our family that the world of creation and its Creator first entered our lives. They taught us how to love God and our neighbors as ourselves.

But our loves soon divided—to likes, dislikes, true loves and hates. And thus we saw the world as it really is. We saw the war of life—divided pathways: some people choosing the hills of ambition without the roads of justice; some, the marshes of pleasure without the land of temperance; and some, choosing the way of the Lord, wherever it led.

This must be our way. Whether we be-

come housewife, career woman, or Sister, we all have one thing in common—our vocation to love—to love God, directly and through others. It is only for us to choose which way to direct this love.

Each of us, sooner or later, asks "But which for me?" And with that question comes the three-road answer: married, single or religious life—each adaptable to fulfilling the primary object of our birth.

The focal point of married life is love. Sharing the things of God, husband and wife live fruitfully in His service.

His service can be the aim, also, of every career woman. She can promote the activities of this earth in His name.

His name should be the work and word of every Sister, dedicated to Him in an intimate way. Her goal should be to promote the perfection of His creation in herself and in all those she comes in contact with.

In any life we choose we'll find love's familiar partner, sacrifice. And love through sacrifice will bring consummation to an eternal birth in love.

—Sister Victor Marie, O.S.F.

The Interlude, February 24, 1962. Image courtesy of the Laverne and Dorothy Brown Library Archives, University of St. Francis, Joliet, IL.

Made in the USA
Monee, IL
07 October 2020